Responsive Classroom®

THE
Language
OF Learning

Teaching Students Core Thinking, Listening, and Speaking Skills

Margaret Berry Wilson

Foreword by Lora M. Hodges, EdD

NORTHEAST FOUNDATION FOR CHILDREN, INC.

All net proceeds from the sale of this book support the work of Northeast Foundation for Children, Inc. (NEFC). NEFC, a not-for-profit educational organization, is the developer of the *Responsive Classroom*® approach to teaching.

The stories in this book are all based on real events. However, in order to respect the privacy of students, names and many identifying characteristics of students and situations have been changed.

ISBN: 978-1-892989-61-1
Library of Congress Control Number: 2013948506

Cover and book design by Helen Merena
Cover photograph © Jeff Woodward. All rights reserved.
Interior photographs © Alice Proujansky, Jeff Woodward, Peter Wrenn, and Vermont Films Group. All rights reserved.

Thanks to the teachers and students who welcomed Northeast Foundation for Children to take photos in their classrooms.

Northeast Foundation for Children, Inc.
85 Avenue A, P.O. Box 718
Turners Falls, MA 01376-0718

800-360-6332
www.responsiveclassroom.org

CONTENTS

FOREWORD by Lora M. Hodges, EdD, Executive Director,
Northeast Foundation for Children   v

INTRODUCTION ▪ The Power of Student Conversation   1

CHAPTER 1 ▪ Listening Essentials   4

CHAPTER 2 ▪ Speaking Essentials 38

CHAPTER 3 ▪ Asking and Answering Questions 68

CHAPTER 4 ▪ Crafting an Argument 100

CHAPTER 5 ▪ The Art of Agreeing and Disagreeing 134

CONCLUSION ▪ Letting Students Shine 170

APPENDIX A ▪ Quick Guide to the Teaching Techniques
Used in This Book 172

APPENDIX B ▪ Suggested Timeline—When to Teach
Speaking and Listening Skills 191

FURTHER RESOURCES 193

ACKNOWLEDGMENTS 198

INDEX 201

Students enter our school doors with a vision of themselves as learners, filled with hopes and dreams for learning. That's what I firmly believe. With them, they bring an innate curiosity and a thirst to discover words, numbers, music, and art; to hear, tell, and make meaning of stories from the past and stories that are yet unfolding; to explore the wonders of faraway planets and uncover the marvels of the one named Earth—and most importantly, to learn all the nitty-gritty details of whatever captures their own interests and helps to manifest their hidden gifts and talents.

It is their expectation that school will give them opportunities to develop their own ideas about facts, discover how things work, invent and innovate, put new skills into use, develop self-confidence, make good decisions, learn to play well with others, connect with classmates, and have fun doing so.

As their teachers, we hold in our hearts our own hopes and dreams for them, too. We want them to engage in academic rigor and to be ideamongers who contribute to classroom learning—and we also want them to become the very best people they can be; to live the very best lives they can live; and to contribute as best they can to their families, schools, communities, and our world. Ultimately, what we hope they learn from us is—at its core—the stuff they'll need for a satisfying and successful life. But to learn all that, students must master what is essentially a new language—the language of learning.

There is a universal language that all schools have, regardless of their unique school culture. Much more than speech, this language of learning is a set of concrete skills and strategies for thinking, then speaking; for listening, then thinking; for translating curiosity into well-thought-out questions; for building on others' ideas; and taking a conversation and train of thought to higher and higher levels. We may, at times, assume that students will somehow access and naturally develop fluency in the language of learning and therefore won't need us to name it, much less teach it.

Yet, achieving fluency in the language of learning does not automatically happen for children. We must deliberately help them master the set of requisite skills and socially shared conventions and expectations that advances high-quality learning. This book will help you do just that by giving you practical tools and resources to move your students toward fluency in five core competencies:

- ⇢ **listening with respect and for understanding**

- ⇢ **speaking clearly, concisely, and confidently**

- ⇢ **asking purposeful questions—and answering them succinctly and appropriately**

- ⇢ **using sound reasons and evidence to make an argument**

- ⇢ **agreeing and disagreeing respectfully to advance powerful exchanges of ideas**

Children have always needed these competencies in order to be highly engaged, self-motivated thinkers, doers, creators, and learners. Moreover, a student's mastery of these competencies is foundational for reaching the rigor inherent in the Common Core State Standards and for successfully navigating our rapidly changing global community. The content, strategies, and resources presented in this book will help you teach, coach, and encourage students in developing and demonstrating these competencies.

And yes, these skill sets can be challenging for students to master. Make no doubt about it, we ourselves will at times need to develop new mindsets and flex new teaching muscles to teach these skills effectively. But I have faith in every child's ability to learn them well and every teacher's ability to teach them well. So I invite you to roll up your sleeves and dive into this worthy work. After all, our teaching is more rewarding when we face challenges with our students, hurdle over the obstacles together, and enjoy the rewards of progress, big and small.

This book's content and strategies for teaching the language of learning are integral to the *Responsive Classroom*®, a research-based approach to teaching that enables educators to create engaging academics for every child, build a positive learning community, and manage classrooms effectively. As leader of the organization behind this approach, I thoroughly enjoyed watching a bright nugget of an idea for this book become a reality. I'm confident that this book will serve you well for many years to come. It's exciting to envision all our children across the nation becoming fluent and highly competent in the language of learning and in developing the critical skills they need for success today, tomorrow, and far into the future.

Lora M. Hodges, EdD
Executive Director
Northeast Foundation for Children

THE

Language
OF **Learning**

Teaching Students
Core Thinking, Listening,
and Speaking Skills

The Power of Student Conversation

"By giving our students practice in talking with others,
we give them frames for thinking on their own."

—LEV VYGOTSKY

While I was observing a third grade class recently, a lively conversation captured my attention. The students were discussing Thomas Rockwell's book *How to Eat Fried Worms*. In the book, two boys, Alan and Joe, bet another, Billy, that he won't be able to eat fifteen worms in fifteen days. When it appears that Billy will accomplish this feat, the boys resort to trickery to try and stop him. After reading aloud one of these tricks, the teacher paused and asked a seemingly simple question, "Is tricking someone cheating?"

At first, many students, clearly empathizing with Billy, thought the other boys' tricks definitely constituted cheating. They laid out a strong case that by resorting to sneaky tactics, Alan and Joe were being unfair and dishonest. Then, one student wondered aloud if what Alan and Joe did was similar to "the special moves I do in soccer that help me get past the other team. Those moves are kind of tricks, but they're not against the rules. So they aren't cheating."

His classmates were silent for a moment as they considered this new viewpoint. Another student spoke up and said, "I agree with you part of the way. I think soccer

1

can help us figure this out. But, I'm wondering, is what they did more like what you're saying or more like an illegal soccer move?" The teacher let the class wrestle with these ideas a bit longer before moving on to the next point of discussion.

It was clear to me that this conversation helped the children better understand the book's characters. But after further reflection, I realized that it also gave them meaningful practice with the critical speaking and thinking skills they would need to analyze and discuss more complex texts and real-life situations. This book is designed to help you teach your students these types of skills—the ones they'll need to have for the same kinds of challenging, thought-provoking academic conversations.

The teaching techniques described in this book are based on the *Responsive Classroom* approach to teaching and learning. Since its inception in 1981, *Responsive Classroom* has recognized the importance of teaching children listening, speaking, and thinking skills—and has been giving teachers tools for explicitly doing that teaching. Numerous other national organizations and initiatives have also come to recognize the importance of explicitly teaching speaking and listening:

→ The Common Core State Standards include speaking and listening skills as critical skills students must learn to be college- and career-ready.

→ The Partnership for 21st Century Skills has similarly recognized the importance of academic communication skills to students' future success.

→ The National Council of Teachers of Mathematics (NCTM), National Council of Teachers of English (NCTE), National Science Teachers Association (NSTA), and National Council for the Social Studies (NCSS) all emphasize communication skills as critical for success in their content areas.

These and numerous other initiatives and organizations recognize that students who can listen deeply, reflect on what others are saying, express their ideas clearly and persuasively, ask insightful questions, and debate respectfully will be more successful in school and outside of school—and be more likely to grow into thoughtful, caring citizens.

Of course, students don't enter the classroom knowing all the ins and outs of how to hold productive conversations. They need to be taught specifically how to make their talk:

- **Clear and coherent**—expressing ideas in ways that are to the point and easy for their classmates to understand.

- **Purposeful**—coming to conversations prepared, thinking before speaking, and having a clear purpose when speaking, such as to assert a different opinion, ask a question, or clarify understanding.

- **Well-reasoned**—supporting their assertions and opinions with relevant reasons, facts, and other evidence.

- **Conveying curiosity and open-mindedness**—listening with genuine interest to others' ideas and thoughtfully considering a wide range of perspectives.

- **Respectful**—speaking and listening in ways that always show consideration for others.

This book offers you practical techniques for teaching children how to have academic conversations that reflect all of these characteristics. It also gives you ideas for seamlessly integrating this teaching into your regular curriculum.

You'll walk away with a roadmap for teaching children the essentials of speaking and listening—and for stimulating powerful classroom conversations that put every student on the path to academic success.

Note: In this book, for ease of reading, the term "parent" is used to represent all the caregivers involved in a child's life.

Listening Essentials

Quiet, Focused, Comprehending

Successful academic conversations begin with listening. To engage in productive talk with classmates, students must first hear and understand what another person says. Children need to learn all aspects of listening—from quieting themselves and giving their full attention to the speaker, to paraphrasing and summarizing to make sure they understood what was said, and all the critical steps in between.

Being a capable listener has far-reaching benefits. Students who listen well can learn more from their teachers and develop stronger relationships with their classmates and others. Picture this typical scene from a third grade classroom as students investigate different ways to solve double-digit multiplication problems.

Cheri describes how she tried to solve the problem 14 x 23: "I broke up the first number. I multiplied 10 times 23 and got 230. Then, I tried 4 x 23, but that was kind of hard for me. So, I did 4 x 20, which is 80, and 4 x 3, which is 12. But then I got confused and time was up. I could use everyone's help now."

CHAPTER

1

Common Core Connections · · · · · · · 7

How to Teach the Skills:

   Focusing Attention · · · · · · · · · · · 12
   Showing Interest · · · · · · · · · · · · · 17
   Sustaining Attention · · · · · · · · · · 20
   Developing Comprehension · · · · 25

Giving Meaningful Feedback · · · · 30

Addressing Common Mistakes · · · 33

Essential Skills at a Glance · · · · · · · 36

Sample Letter to Parents · · · · · · · · 37

As Cheri speaks, she makes notes of what she did on the whiteboard. Her classmates have their eyes on her and the board. Many lean forward and scrunch up their faces, trying to figure out her approach.

Two classmates respond to what they heard. Max asks, "So you tried to break the numbers into tens and ones, the way we do for addition, right?" When Cheri nods, he says, "And you got 230, 80, and 12, right?" Cheri says, "Right again." Then Sara says, "So I think you should just add those three numbers up, and then you'll have the answer."

Max's and Sara's keen attention and listening were critical—both to their understanding of Cheri's method and to helping her use it successfully.

In this chapter, you'll learn more about why the listening skills these students demonstrated are so essential. You'll also learn concrete steps for helping students develop the skills required for listening—from focusing their attention to truly thinking about what a speaker said.

Why These Skills Matter

All students, even those who initially struggle, need to and can learn how to listen at school. Teaching listening skills enables students to:

- **Engage more fully in conversations with others.** Before students can add to what someone else has said, ask questions or answer them, agree or disagree, they have to hear and understand what was said.

- **Better understand academic material presented orally.** From brief mini-lessons to lectures, from test directions to homework assignments, teachers often convey information to students orally. The better students listen, the more information they'll retain, understand, and put to use. In addition, some listening comprehension skills, such as paraphrasing and summarizing, correlate directly with skills required for academic work in content areas such as reading, social studies, and science.

- **Develop stronger relationships with classmates.** Effective listening is crucial for building strong peer relationships that enable collaborative learning. To learn well together, students need to take multiple perspectives and develop empathy for one another—and that begins with listening.

Common Core Connections

Kindergarten	**SL.K.1:** Participate in collaborative conversations with diverse partners about kindergarten topics and texts.
	SL.K.1a: Follow agreed-upon rules for discussions (e.g., listening to others and taking turns speaking).
	SL.K.2: Confirm understanding of a text read aloud or information presented orally or through other media by asking and answering questions about key details and requesting clarification if something is not understood.
	SL.K.3: Ask and answer questions in order to seek help, get information, or clarify something that is not understood.
	SL.K.6: Speak audibly.
1st Grade	**SL.1.1:** Participate in collaborative conversations with diverse partners about grade 1 topics and texts.
	SL.1.1a: Follow agreed-upon rules for discussions (e.g., listening to others with care, speaking one at a time).
	SL.1.1c: Ask questions to clear up any confusion about the topics and texts under discussion.
	SL.1.3: Ask and answer questions about what a speaker says in order to gather additional information or clarify something that is not understood.
	SL.1.6: Produce complete sentences when appropriate to task and situation.
2nd Grade	**SL.2.1:** Participate in collaborative conversations with diverse partners about grade 2 topics and texts.
	SL.2.1a: Follow agreed-upon rules for discussions (e.g., gaining the floor in respectful ways, listening to others with care, speaking one at a time).
	SL.2.1c: Ask for clarification and further explanation as needed about the topics and texts under discussion.

2nd Grade, cont.	**SL.2.3:** Ask and answer questions about what a speaker says in order to clarify comprehension, gather additional information, or deepen understanding. **SL.2.6:** Produce complete sentences when appropriate to task and situation in order to provide requested detail or clarification.
3rd Grade	**SL.3.1:** Engage effectively in a range of collaborative discussions (one-on-one, in groups, and teacher-led) with diverse partners on grade 3 topics and texts. **SL.3.1b:** Follow agreed-upon rules for discussions (e.g., gaining the floor in respectful ways, listening to others with care, speaking one at a time). **SL.3.1c:** Ask questions to check understanding of information presented. **SL.3.3:** Ask and answer questions about information from a speaker. **SL.3.6:** Speak in complete sentences when appropriate to task and situation in order to provide requested detail or clarification.
4th Grade	**SL.4.1:** Engage effectively in a range of collaborative discussions (one-on-one, in groups, and teacher-led) with diverse partners on grade 4 topics and texts. **SL.4.1b:** Follow agreed-upon rules for discussions and carry out assigned roles. **SL.4.1c:** Pose and respond to specific questions to clarify or follow up on information. **SL.4.2:** Paraphrase portions of a text read aloud or information presented in diverse media and formats. **SL.4.6:** Differentiate between contexts that call for formal English and situations where informal discourse is appropriate; use formal English when appropriate to task and situation.

Speaking and Listening Standards Supported in Chapter One

5th Grade

SL.5.1: Engage effectively in a range of collaborative discussions (one-on-one, in groups, and teacher-led) with diverse partners on grade 5 topics and texts.

SL.5.1b: Follow agreed-upon rules for discussions and carry out assigned roles.

SL.5.1c: Pose and respond to specific questions.

SL.5.2: Summarize a written text read aloud or information presented in diverse media and formats.

L.5.3: Summarize the points a speaker makes.

SL.5.6: Adapt speech to a variety of contexts and tasks, using formal English when appropriate to task and situation.

6th Grade

SL.6.1: Engage effectively in a range of collaborative discussions (one-on-one, in groups, and teacher-led) with diverse partners on grade 6 topics and texts.

SL.6.1b: Follow rules for collegial discussions.

SL.6.1c: Pose and respond to specific questions.

SL.6.1d: Review the key ideas expressed and demonstrate understanding of multiple perspectives through reflection and paraphrasing.

SL.6.6: Adapt speech to a variety of contexts and tasks, demonstrating command of formal English when indicated or appropriate.

How to Teach the Skills

As you teach students the essentials of listening, remember to:

→ **Show faith in students' abilities to grow as listeners.** Some children come to us with more fully developed listening skills than others, so it can be easy to assume that some students are inherently good listeners and others are not. Resist that trap! Even children who interrupt, forget what others said, or lose focus can learn these skills. Try to meet students where they are, while holding on to the belief that they can improve and get to where they need to be.

→ **Keep developmental considerations in mind.** Children's development can greatly influence their ability to listen. For instance, in first grade children tend to go through a verbal growth spurt and can be quite talkative. They may initially need to listen for shorter periods of time and have more frequent opportunities to talk.

→ **Think about children's cultural backgrounds.** For example, in some cultures making eye contact is a sign of disrespect, yet our job as teachers is to prepare students to succeed in the larger culture in which they will live and work. If you're teaching skills that might conflict with a child's home culture, such as making eye contact when listening, present these skills as ones that can support success in school, college, and the workplace. Be patient—these students may need more time than their classmates to put these skills to use.

Four key listening skills

✔ **Focusing attention**

✔ **Showing interest**

✔ **Sustaining attention**

✔ **Developing comprehension**

➜ **Begin with basic skills and add more complex ones throughout the year.** Certain listening skills are critical to teach starting on the first day of school (especially how and when to keep quiet). Begin with these skills, and then gradually add in new ones as they're needed and as children are ready for greater complexity or challenge.

➜ **Model listening skills.** Students often learn best by watching us, so be sure that you also use the same listening skills you're teaching. Try to listen with your full attention, remember key details from conversations, and avoid interrupting.

In the pages that follow, I outline ideas for how to teach listening skills so that students can build their listening stamina and abilities. Focus on the most basic listening skills during the first lessons. Then move on to teach more advanced listening skills.

Knowing how to turn voices off promptly is one of the first lessons I teach a new class. After all, it's impossible to do any of the work of school until children can be quiet and focus on you for information or directions or on classmates during class discussions.

For a suggested timeline of when to teach academic conversation skills throughout the school year, see page 191.

FOCUSING ATTENTION

We teachers often think of listening as an internal skill, involving communication between the ears and the brain. For children, though, listening begins with its outward physical manifestations, and children need to learn how to physically demonstrate listening so that they can start to actually listen.

These basic but fundamental listening skills are responding promptly to signals for quiet attention; keeping voices off, bodies calm, and eyes on the speaker; and waiting until the speaker has completely finished before signaling a desire to talk. Even students in upper elementary grades need support learning and practicing how to listen well.

Responding Promptly to Signals for Quiet Attention

Introduce the skill. Students won't automatically know when you expect them to listen. You can use Interactive Modeling (page 172) to teach them how to respond to an auditory signal (such as a chime) when they're spread out around the room *and* to a visual signal (such as a raised hand) when you need to get their attention in a smaller area.

Before you teach this lesson, think about exactly what you expect from your students. Consider:

→ how quickly you want them to respond to your signal

→ whether they should "freeze" if they are moving about

→ whether their hands should be empty (and not touching materials)

→ how they should help those who aren't responding to your signal

Once you're clear on what you expect and will model, introduce your lesson by letting students know why it's important to respond to these signals quickly:

> "Sometimes I'll need to get your attention quickly so I can give you important information or the next set of directions. At those times, I'll ring the chime. I'm going to show you what to do when you hear it. Watch what I do when Kayla rings the chime."

Practice the skill. Over the first few days, have students practice responding to your signals on multiple occasions. Be sure to give them positive feedback each time they're successful.

> "That time, everyone was still and looking at me within five seconds. You're really taking care of each other's learning!"

The more automatically students respond to signals, the more focused and ready to listen they'll be.

Activities and games can also be a fun and powerful way to bolster students' abilities to respond quickly to signals for quiet attention. For instance, play the Freeze Game, in which you play music and children freeze when it stops and stay frozen until it starts again.

Provide ongoing support. Younger students and some older ones may need the support of an anchor chart listing the key expectations for responding to signals. Some students may still struggle, so consider helping them by:

↝ **having private practice time** with them

↝ **assigning a buddy to help them** remember key aspects of responding to signals

> Listening
> * Voices off
> * Eyes on speaker
> * Body calm, facing speaker
> * Give speaker your whole attention

↝ **giving them more explicit and frequent feedback** (for instance, by making a check mark on a recording sheet every time they respond and periodically showing them the sheet privately)

Voices Off, Bodies Calm, Eyes on Speaker

Introduce the skills. After teaching students how to respond to the signals for quiet attention, you can use Interactive Modeling (page 172) to teach this next set of skills involved in listening. In this lesson:

→ **Continue laying the groundwork** for why listening well matters:

> "Being a good listener shows respect. It also helps us learn. Right now, notice what I do with my voice, body, and eyes while I listen."

→ **Demonstrate (without narration),** being sure students point out that your voice was off, body was still and turned toward the speaker, and eyes were on the speaker. As students notice each skill, follow up with a question to help highlight why that particular aspect is important. For instance, if a student notices you were silent, you might ask:

> "Why is it important that we keep our voices off when someone else is talking?"

Although these "smaller" skills of listening may seem obvious to us, they don't come naturally to many students. The more they can understand the purpose of the skills and see each of them in action, the more likely they are to learn and master them.

→ **Immediately let students practice.** After you and a few students have demonstrated, let all students practice these skills just as you taught them. Remember to give them prompt feedback about how they're doing.

Provide additional practice and ongoing support. Over the first days and weeks of school, give students multiple opportunities to practice:

→ **In whole-group lessons and partner chats.** Remind students of the basic listening expectations before whole-group discussions or one-on-one conversations:

> "Who can remind us of what our voices, faces, and bodies should be doing while others are speaking?"

↝ **At morning meetings and other class gatherings.** These social times can provide great opportunities to practice listening skills. For instance, have students greet each other, reminding them to focus and listen as they're greeted. Or, as students share personal news, connect back to what you've already taught about listening.

> "Remember to give speakers your whole attention—eyes, bodies, minds."

↝ **Through a variety of interactive structures.** Keep the practice interesting by varying the ways you have students speak and listen. For instance, try Inside-Outside Circles, Four Corners, or Maître d', giving students interesting topics to discuss and frequent reminders and reinforcement about listening. (See pages 177–186 for more on these and other practice structures.)

↝ **Through games.** Make listening practice fun by occasionally playing games that require listening and attention. For instance, have students toss a ball in a circle. The group should quickly shift its focus and show listening to the person who catches the ball. That person speaks, perhaps sharing a favorite of some type, for instance, "My favorite color is blue." Everyone repeats what she says, and then she throws the ball to a new person.

As students are starting to put these listening skills to use, point out their successes and efforts.

> "I saw so many people turning toward Angela when she shared her news. Your voices were off and your eyes were on her. That helped all of us focus on what she said."

Waiting Until the Speaker
Has Completely Finished

Introduce the skill. When students wave their hands to speak while someone else is talking, it's distracting and disrespectful to the speaker. Waving hands also prevents the children themselves from fully listening to the speaker. Use a think-aloud embedded within an Interactive Modeling lesson (page 172) to teach students to hold their own thoughts "inside" and wait until a speaker has finished before signaling their desire to talk. During your lesson, emphasize:

→ **The importance of focus while listening.** Teaching students to hold off on their own comments is an important beginning step in teaching complete listening. You might tell students:

> "When someone else is speaking, we need to give them our complete attention. That means we try to think only about what they're saying. I'm going to show you what that looks like."

→ **What total attention looks like.** Invite a student to begin describing a book he's reading while you demonstrate how to keep your focus while listening. Afterwards, tell students what you were thinking while the student was talking. For example, with older students you might say something like this:

> "When Wendi first said the title, I almost raised my hand so I could say, 'Oh, I've read that book.' But I wanted to hear what she thought, so I stayed quiet until she was done."

For younger students, you may want to make this think-aloud simpler and more concrete by using a paper thought-bubble attached to a craft stick.

→ **Reflecting on the strategies you used for self-control.** Ask students:

> "What did you see me doing to give Wendi my full attention and learn as much as I could from her?"

Make sure students notice that you listened to Wendi's words, stopped yourself from raising your hand, and remained silent so you could keep listening to her.

Practice the skill. Give students multiple chances to practice the skill of listening to everything a speaker has to say in whole-group discussions, partner chats, Swap Meets, and other interactive structures (pages 177–186). Frequently have students reflect on their progress with this skill.

> "I noticed many of you exercising patience and listening fully just as we've been practicing. How are you remembering to give your complete attention and keep from interrupting?"

Provide ongoing support. For younger students or classes where interrupting is common, you may want to use a talking stick to visibly designate the speaker. A talking stick can help students maintain their focus on the speaker and refrain from speaking until the stick reaches them.

Another effective technique is providing a certain amount of wait time between speakers. For instance, have students slowly count to three in their heads after someone finishes speaking before raising hands or contributing.

SHOWING INTEREST

Once students have the basics of listening down, it's time to go deeper. For younger students, this learning may not occur until mid-year. Older students who have had more experience with listening may be ready for these lessons within the first few weeks of school. All students need to learn that being a supportive listener requires more than just being quiet and having voices off. The key ways to show interest are:

⤳ **leaning toward the speaker**

⤳ **using supportive facial expressions, such as smiling or nodding**

⤳ **occasionally making respectful sounds**

Children need to understand that supportive listeners are not always completely still or silent. When a speaker says something touching, a listener might say, "Ah," or when someone tells a sad story, a listener might make a sad face to show empathy.

Younger students, who tend to be more concrete in their thinking, may need you to break the skills of showing interest into chunks and teach each one separately. Older students can often learn them as a complete skill set in one lesson. However you decide to teach these skills, realize that they come more easily to some students than to others, and be patient as they learn.

Introduce the skill. Writers' workshop can be an opportune time to include the teaching of listening, as students' writing often benefits from oral sharing of stories. Here's how Mrs. Johnson, a third grade teacher, uses an Expert Demonstration (page 175) to teach how to show interest as part of a writers' workshop lesson.

→ **Set the stage for the lesson.** After gathering the class around the circle, Mrs. Johnson says:

> "Today, we'll begin working on our personal narratives.
> I've invited some former students who are now in the sixth grade to share about personal narratives and demonstrate what it looks like to be a respectful listener who encourages the speaker."

→ **Assign observation tasks.** Mrs. Johnson has one of the sixth graders talk about his personal narrative while the other demonstrators listen with interest. She tells the third graders to watch for elements of supportive listening:

> "Watch how the listeners use their faces, bodies,
> and sounds to show the speaker that they're interested
> and want to listen to everything he or she has to say."

→ **Have experts demonstrate briefly.** While the sixth graders demonstrate, Mrs. Johnson silently observes along with the third graders. (Before this demonstration, she had prepared the sixth grade modelers. She had them choose a short personal narrative that would resonate with third graders and she reviewed with them how to be supportive listeners.)

→ **After the demonstration, ask open-ended questions.** Mrs. Johnson gives the third graders a moment to reflect on what they observed. Then she asks them:

> "How did José show Tadashi that he was really listening
> to the story of how Tadashi got stitches in his forehead?"

Recognizing that too much "encouragement" might take attention away from the speaker, she also asked:

> "How did José make sure he wasn't being disruptive or taking away from the story?"

Practice the skill. You can have students practice supportive listening by using partner structures, such as turning and talking with a partner or Inside-Outside Circles (page 180). Because supportive listening often involves personal reactions and gestures, children may find it easier to practice these skills in more private settings. Pair students up to discuss interesting topics, have them spread out around the room, and monitor their use of the skills by walking around and providing coaching and positive feedback.

Provide ongoing support. You can use anchor charts to highlight key aspects of supportive listening. In addition:

> We encourage speakers by:
> * Leaning forward
> * Nodding or smiling
> * Showing surprise
> * Showing empathy
> * Laughing quietly (at funny parts)

→ **Reinforce students' efforts frequently.** Sometimes students may feel awkward and unnatural using these skills, so they need to hear what they're doing well and that their efforts are worth it.

> "Layana, when you were listening to Malachi's story, I saw your shoulders go up and shiver when he talked about the spider he found in his bed. You showed him that you had empathy for how he felt without interrupting him."

→ **Do additional teaching.** Some students have a harder time being expressive with their faces or bodies, so be patient as they learn. Support their growth by giving extra instruction and practice, either to the whole group or to them privately.

→ **Sit with students during a partner conversation.** This way, you can demonstrate supportive listening live and in the moment.

SUSTAINING ATTENTION

Another way to go deeper with listening is to help students focus on what to do internally while they listen so that they can maintain their attention on the speaker and gain understanding. We all know that we can look like we're listening when our thoughts are actually miles away. The key attention-sustaining skills to teach students are focusing on the speaker's words, tone, and body language; listening for key details; and refocusing if attention wanders.

Focusing on the Speaker's Words, Tone, and Body Language

Introduce the skills. You can use a think-aloud technique within an Interactive Modeling lesson (page 172) to help students understand what it "looks" like to analyze a speaker's words, tone, and body language so they can understand his main message and emotions.

↝ **Tie this lesson in to what you've already taught about reading.**

> "When we read, we try to figure out the main idea. We do the same thing when we're listening. As I listen to Farrah, I'm going to notice her words, tone of voice, and body language. After she finishes, I'll use a think-aloud to tell you what I was thinking."

↝ **Have the speaker talk briefly.** Recommend she talk about a topic that she has an emotional connection to, such as excitement about a family event or something that's been challenging for her in math.

↝ **As the student shares, demonstrate sustaining attention.** Be sure to model the skills you've already taught (such as eyes on speaker, leaning in, and appreciative sounds) exactly the way you want students to show them.

↝ **Do a think-aloud to "show" your thought process.**

> "I heard Farrah say that she's having a hard time learning to multiply fractions. I figured out this was her main idea. I could also tell from her earnest tone and the way she scrunched up her face that she's trying hard to figure out how to do this."

Then ask students what they noticed about how you listened and what sorts of things you paid attention to. Be sure they notice the key aspects of what you did—that you first tried to determine the main point, paid attention to Farrah's tone, and tried to read her body language.

→ **Invite a student volunteer to listen to you.** Recount a brief anecdote about a challenge you faced as a student. Then have the listening student point out your main idea and whatever she learned from watching your body language. Next, ask the rest of the class what they noticed about how this student demonstrated sustained attention.

→ **Have students work in groups of three or four.** In each group, one person speaks, one listens, and one or two observe the listener (and can take notes), and then they alternate roles.

Provide ongoing practice and support. Staying tuned in to a speaker's words, tone, and body language is challenging and complex. Students may need multiple lessons and plenty of practice to learn this skill set. As students practice, point out their successful efforts.

> "I saw many of you making sure you zeroed in on what your partners were saying and how they felt about it. You are learning to pay attention to speakers."

You can also use an anchor chart to help students remember how to pay attention as others speak.

Listeners pay attention to a speaker's:

* Words—What's the main topic?

* Tone—What emotions are being expressed?

* Body language—What emotions are being expressed?

Look for opportunities to reinforce these lessons. For instance, when guest speakers come to assemblies, remind students to use the skills they've been learning. Debrief with them afterwards about how they did. Or, in connection with a social studies lesson, show students brief clips from the news so they can practice picking up on nonverbal cues (body language, tone of voice) and verbal cues (word choice).

Listening for Key Details

Introduce the skill. Once students have had some experience listening for the "big picture," they need to learn to tune in to the details of what speakers are saying. Again, you can use Interactive Modeling with a think-aloud to make this complex skill accessible for students. In your lesson:

→ **Highlight why this skill matters.** Tie this skill in to what students have been learning academically.

> "Today, we're going to learn how listeners make sense of what someone is saying by taking note of the important details they share. This kind of listening is a lot like what we've discussed in reading and in social studies. Watch and see how I do this after Chris shares about a story he's been writing."

→ **Use the think-aloud to offer techniques for remembering.**

> "While Chris was talking, I remembered to think about the big picture—his story is a mystery. Then I heard some important details. I used my fingers to mark three of them. First, the detectives are a fourth grade girl and boy. Second, the mystery is that someone keeps stealing lunches out of lockers. Third, they're making a list of suspects."

Provide ongoing practice and support. One way to do this is to speak for just a minute or so on a topic related to a current unit of study. Then pause and have students briefly discuss with partners (who you've assigned in advance) what they noticed. Next, have them talk about aspects they've previously learned: main idea, tone, and body language. Finally, have them each name what they think were the three most important details that you shared. Repeat the practice a few times.

When most students seem ready, have them practice with a partner while you observe and coach. Paired Verbal Fluency (page 182) can be especially effective for this practice.

→ One student is A; the other is B.

→ Give an interesting topic for discussion, such as how they're planning to end a story they're writing, which strategy they're using to solve a math problem and why, or what they like about a passage they just read for social studies.

→ Student A speaks on the topic for about one minute. Remind B that his job is to watch and notice A's main idea, tone, body language, and key details. Give B thirty seconds to describe these to A.

→ A and B switch roles and repeat the exercise.

→ Each then has thirty seconds to respond to what the other said.

As you circulate, point out what students are doing well.

> "Traci, I noticed that you picked up on how excited Justin was about space from the way he was making his eyes bigger and gesturing with his hands. You also remembered three important details he mentioned."

Refocusing If Attention Wanders

Introduce the skill. From time to time, any listener may briefly lose focus. But effective listeners know how to refocus their attention on the speaker. For students, knowing how to do this quickly is essential to ensuring that their learning stays on track. To teach these refocusing skills, you can use a Fishbowl or Expert Demonstration (pages 174–175). Here are some tips:

→ **Set a purpose:**

> "You're all honing your listening skills. I've seen you sustaining your attention for longer and longer periods of time. But everyone occasionally gets distracted while listening. We're going to learn skills to help us refocus and respectfully find out what we missed."

→ **Choose a few demonstrators and practice with them in advance.** Make sure they can show some concrete ways to refocus, such as sitting up straighter or asking the speaker to repeat her last point.

→ **After the demonstration, debrief.** During this whole-group discussion, prompt the demonstrators to share what they were thinking as they used various techniques to refocus on the speaker. For instance, you might ask, "Charlie, when you sat up straighter, can you tell us about your thinking then?" The student might respond, "I realized I wasn't listening and sat up straighter to kind of wake my brain up again."

Provide ongoing support. Unlike most other speaking and listening skills, you wouldn't want to have students practice refocusing because you don't want to encourage them to become distracted. However, you can remind them to put these skills to use if they do lose focus while engaging in academic conversations. To create an anchor chart for support, brainstorm with students some early warning signs that they're losing focus.

Signs of Losing Focus

* Are you **looking** around the room?
* Are you **playing** with something?
* Are you **forgetting** what the person just said?
* Are you **thinking** of something else?

Then post some examples of language students can use to respectfully ask a speaker to repeat information they may have missed.

Sorry, I missed your last point. Could you say that again?

I spaced for a minute. Could you go back to the part when you said ____?

I heard ____, but I missed what you said after that.

DEVELOPING LISTENING COMPREHENSION

The ultimate test for listeners is whether the speaker feels heard and understood. But figuring out what speakers are really saying is a challenge. The essential skills listeners need for comprehension are refraining from thinking about their own ideas, and paraphrasing, summarizing, and checking in.

Refraining From Thinking About Their Own Ideas

Introduce the skill. One of the hardest skills for listeners to learn is to make sure they accurately understand what a speaker has said before they start evaluating whether they agree or disagree, or have a connection to make or question to ask. In some ways, you'll begin this teaching when you demonstrate how to wait to raise hands to speak until someone has finished. But students need to have this self-monitoring skill fully fleshed out in a lesson of its own.

You can use Interactive Modeling (page 172) with a think-aloud for this lesson and connect it with an academic activity where staying focused on what someone else is saying is essential to learning. For instance, when students are sharing math strategies, as in this chapter's opening story, understanding what their classmates did is especially important. Otherwise, they won't reap the benefits of their classmates' thinking. For this lesson to be most effective:

→ **Say why this skill is important for their learning.**

> "I'm going to listen to Ben describe how he solved the problem about how to share nine pizzas equally with 18 students. I want to make sure I understand exactly what Ben did before I share what I did because he might have ideas I didn't consider."

→ **Highlight previously taught listening skills as well as the new ones.**

> "From Ben's body language, I saw his confidence in his strategy. When I heard him say he used cubes, I started to think about using cubes, but I reminded myself to refocus. When he said that he got stumped trying to divide the cubes, I wanted to say, 'Me, too,' but again, I told myself to refocus on him to hear what he did next."

Provide ongoing practice and support. Remind students of this skill frequently as you send them off to have discussions, particularly if the topics or questions are challenging. For instance:

→ **When students are sharing personal stories** at a morning meeting or writers' workshop, listeners can easily start making personal or "Me, too" connections. Ask them to hold off on thinking of these connections until the speaker is completely finished.

→ **During lively exchanges**—for example, in a round of Pros and Cons (page 183)—students are often trying to think of the next point they want to make while others are still speaking. Tell them their primary goal is to first make sure they understand the other person's arguments fully.

→ **When students in pairs are discussing a topic** they are both excited about, finishing each other's sentences or assuming what the person will say next can feel natural. Help students realize that their faces and bodies can show interest and enthusiasm, but they need to actually listen to their partner's words and completely understand what he or she has to say before they share their own thoughts.

Frequently have students reflect on how they're doing with this skill. Because you cannot actually see students self-monitoring, they need to learn to judge for themselves how well they're remembering to hold off on thinking about their own connections and opinions while someone is speaking. After students have a chance to talk to partners, for instance, you might ask:

> "How did you do with holding off on your own ideas? Did anyone have a moment when you had to remind yourself to stay focused on the listener?"

As students share their experiences, validate that it's natural to start forming one's own ideas. Then remind them that we are better able to comprehend speakers when we wait to make sure we fully grasp what they've said.

Paraphrasing, Summarizing, and Checking In

Introduce the skills. First, define paraphrasing (restating what was said in one's own words) and summarizing (giving a brief wrap-up of the speaker's main ideas). Then, because these are challenging skills to learn, you may want to teach each one in a separate lesson, using Fishbowl or Expert Demonstration (pages 174–175). Remember to prepare the modelers or experts in advance and choose an accessible topic for them to discuss, such as a story or poem everyone has read, a historical event they've analyzed, or a mathematical or scientific concept or topic they've studied.

What follows are tips for using a Fishbowl demonstration to introduce paraphrasing. You can then adapt the demonstration for a lesson on summarizing.

→ **Set a purpose for learning to paraphrase.** Connect these skills to other academic tasks, such as retelling what one read or paraphrasing what a story character said. For example:

"Just as effective readers can retell what they read in their own words, effective listeners should also be able to restate what another person said using their own words. Paraphrasing helps us make sure we understand what the speaker is saying and shows them we're listening."

↪ **Remind observers to note how the Fishbowl modelers paraphrased.**

"Watch how the group in the Fishbowl discusses an article we read on animal habitats and uses paraphrasing to make sure they understand the key points others are making. Listen especially for phrases they use to start their paraphrasing and how it helps with the group's understanding."

↪ **As you debrief after the demonstration, call students' attention to key sentence starters for future use.**

What I hear you saying is _____.

Are you saying that _____?

If I heard you correctly, you think _____.

↪ **Then go over how to check in with a speaker.** Checking in can be just a quick question, but it helps students know immediately if their paraphrasing or summaries are accurate. Provide students with quick ways to check in.

What I heard you say was _____, right?

Do I have that right?

Was that your main point?

Practice the skills. Eventually students should paraphrase, summarize, or check in only as needed (unless it's specifically part of their academic work, of course). But while students are learning these skills, have them intentionally practice them in their conversations. An especially helpful practice structure is Numbered Heads Together (page 181), which specifically requires students to summarize. Here's how to adapt this structure, using an example from math, so it can help students practice either paraphrasing or summarizing:

⇢ **Assign students to small groups.** Have students count off in the group.

⇢ **Give the group an engaging math problem to solve.** Tell the group that you might call on anyone in the group to explain the group's strategy. Allow several minutes for students to work on solving the problem. Then, signal for quiet attention.

⇢ **Call out one number.** Each person with that number reports to the whole group by summarizing what his group discussed. For instance, if you called out "Three," students with that number in each group would summarize their group's approach.

⇢ **Repeat,** randomly calling out different numbers each time.

Provide ongoing support. You can support students in developing paraphrasing and summarizing skills by posting sentence starters, such as the examples at left. Also, give students plenty of opportunities to practice with partners, to allow them to combine their recall abilities and double-check their thinking. As you circulate during partner or small-group chats, prompt students to use these skills.

> "Zack, before you share, can you summarize what Angel said? Remember to check in with him afterward to make sure your summary was accurate."

And be sure to give students positive reinforcement as they practice. For instance, after a round of Numbered Heads Together, you might say:

> "I noticed that all the speakers accurately summarized what their groups discussed. I also noticed that when speakers weren't sure about something, they checked in with their group. That's exactly how we make sure we're truly understanding people."

Giving Meaningful Feedback

To grow in their listening skills, students need guidance from their teachers in what they're doing well. They also need to hear where their listening has fallen short and what steps they can take to improve their skills.

LOOK FOR LITTLE SUCCESSES

Provide positive feedback as often as you can. Don't wait for students to perfect all listening skills before giving them positive feedback. Look for those small, but critical, successes and reinforce them. For example, reinforce students' efforts for:

→ **making eye contact and using supportive body posture**, even if students are still struggling with other aspects of listening:

> "I notice everyone is looking at the speaker and leaning forward. That's an important first step in being a listener."

→ **remembering key details,** even if not in the correct sequence:

> "You remembered all the main points of what Kendra said. I bet that made her feel that you were really listening to her."

→ **spontaneous use of listening skills,** even if they don't look exactly as taught:

> "I noticed during lunch that you paraphrased what Leon said about his football game and checked in to make sure you were correct. You were listening carefully to his story."

GIVE FEEDBACK RIGHT AWAY

The more immediate your feedback is, the more impact it will have. Don't wait—as soon as you see success, reinforce it!

→ **Reinforce individuals privately** as soon as you can get them on their own.

> "Andre, I noticed that when you were partnered with Luis, you showed interest by leaning in, nodding, and making eye contact. I bet he really felt heard."

→ **Stop the whole group and reinforce** as soon as you see most children exhibiting the skills they're learning.

> "I saw everyone listening carefully. Your voices were off and your eyes were on the speakers."

BE SPECIFIC

Too much information overloads students; vague or general language confuses them. In either instance, students will be unsure of what they did well. For feedback to have a positive effect on children, home in on exactly what they did well:

Too General	Specific and Descriptive
"Good job, Marc!"	"I noticed you paused before speaking to make sure John was done."
"I like that."	"You remembered to summarize what Ana said before adding your own idea."

SAY WHY IT MATTERS

To help students benefit fully from your feedback, frequently follow up with a brief summary of how the skill they used helped them or the speaker.

"Your face reflected the emotions Jerome shared—worry when something bad was happening and excitement when all ended well. You let him know you were listening and you gained a deeper understanding of the story."

"You summarized what Janeka said so clearly. That showed her that you were listening—and summarizing is a key skill for your own learning."

"All of you remembered three key ideas that your partners shared. Striving to remember what a speaker said helps them feel heard and stretches you to better understand their ideas."

Addressing Common Mistakes

Remember that mistakes are part of the learning process. Just as when learning new academic skills, children will make mistakes as they learn listening skills.

Think of interruptions, not remembering, and misstating what was said as mistakes, not misbehavior. Doing so will allow you to take a teaching stance—and help students get back on track without feeling shamed, worried, or incapable.

Tips for Addressing Mistakes

✔ **Carefully choose** which mistakes to correct. When you do correct students, show faith in their desire to improve.

✔ **Tell students how** to correct the mistake—and give them a chance to do so.

✔ **Use a neutral, respectful tone.** Be brief, so you don't stop the flow of the conversation.

INTERRUPTING THE SPEAKER

Because waiting until the speaker has finished is so challenging, students may interrupt the speaker by calling out, raising or waving their hand, or chatting with a neighbor. If any of these happen, use these strategies to get a student back to respectful listening:

→ **Nonverbally redirect the student.** To a student with her hand up, make eye contact and model by lifting your hand briefly and then putting it down in your lap. To a student who blurts out a comment, a quick finger to your lips can remind him without interrupting the speaker.

→ **Redirect the student by giving her a replacement strategy.** Briefly, quietly, and respectfully let the student know what to do instead.

> "Nick, turn toward Mario."

> "Elaine, voice off. Eyes on Felicity."

> "Lilliana, hand down. Show your full attention to Lorenzo."

USING NEGATIVE BODY LANGUAGE

Many children struggle with using facial expressions and body language to show listening with interest. Students might turn away from the speaker, fail to make eye contact, or even frown at her. To help students build positive body language skills:

→ **Briefly provide the replacement behavior.** Then wait to see the follow-through.

If the student . . .	Try this . . .
isn't making eye contact	Quietly say, "Brianna, eyes." Wait for the student to look at her partner.
has turned away from his partner	Quietly say, "Manny, remember to sit knee-to-knee. Show me how that looks." Then wait and see that he does.
is frowning at the speaker	Quietly say, "Show Tia that you're interested by smiling at her or having a neutral face." Wait for the student to do so.

→ **Establish a private signal.** If a child is struggling with negative body language, use a prearranged nonverbal signal to keep her on track. For instance, if she's frowning at the speaker, you could point to a smile to remind her how to be a supportive listener.

MISUNDERSTANDING
THE SPEAKER

Students sometimes tune out the speaker, only partially hear, or incorrectly remember what another person says. In these moments, you may be tempted to step in to protect the speaker's feelings. Avoid this temptation and instead provide further support for the struggling listener.

→ **Have the student work with a partner.** This can help her to better focus on the speaker so she can more easily remember key points. For instance, if the class is sharing highlights from a research project and practicing remembering one another's highlights, partners could help each other with that listening task before having a whole-group discussion.

→ **Direct the speaker to begin again, and stop her at key points.** Doing so breaks up the listening task into smaller chunks. Struggling listeners are then less likely to get overwhelmed and more likely to maintain their focus. For example, when asking students to share discoveries from a science observation, have the speaker pause after each observation so that the listener needs to paraphrase only one discovery at a time.

→ **Give timely reminders.** For example, if a student forgets to restate what a speaker said to ensure he understood correctly, you might say:

> "Daniel, remember to state back what you heard Juan say before you share your own idea, just as we practiced."

Essential Skills at a Glance

LISTENING	
Focusing Attention (pages 12–17)	→ Respond to signals for quiet attention. → Voices off, bodies calm, eyes on speaker. → Turn toward speaker and make eye contact. → Wait until the speaker has completely finished before making comments or asking questions.
Showing Interest (pages 17–19)	→ Lean toward the speaker. → Use supportive facial expressions, such as smiling, nodding, or using other "matching" facial expressions. → Make occasional, respectful sounds to show interest.
Sustaining Attention (pages 20–25)	→ Focus on the speaker's words, tone, and body language. → Listen for key details. → Refocus if attention wanders. → Refrain from thinking about one's own ideas while someone else is speaking.
Developing Comprehension (pages 25–29)	→ Paraphrase (restate what was said in one's own words). → Summarize (give a brief wrap-up of the speaker's main ideas). → Check in with speaker to see if the paraphrase or summary is accurate.

Sample Letter to Parents

Dear Parents,

All year, I'll be helping students develop a skill that's important for school and life beyond school—listening! This week, we began working on some basic ways we can show that we're listening—voices off, turning toward the speaker, and making eye contact.

Here are a few ways you can help your child practice these skills at home:

- Encourage your child when he or she uses listening skills. At school, I might say, "You were quiet the whole time the speaker was talking. That takes a lot of self-control!"

- Help your child remember to show listening with interest when others are speaking. When they're learning to listen, children may develop habits of interrupting or looking away. If your child does this, gently remind him or her to refocus on the speaker.

- Model respectful listening yourself. Children are always watching us, so we can do some of the best teaching of listening skills by being strong listeners ourselves. (I'm trying to be conscious of doing this at school, too!)

If you have any questions, please contact me. Thank you for supporting your child's learning!

Speaking Essentials

Clear, Concise, Confident

To have productive discussions in all subject areas at school, children need to be able to express ideas clearly and succinctly. The ability to take turns in conversations and speak effectively is also essential for the world beyond school—for social relationships, work collaborations, and formal presentations.

Doing writers' workshop in one fifth grade class, students have been learning how to vividly describe the setting for a fictional story. As part of this learning, their teacher, Mr. Nelson, puts them in small groups to take turns orally describing their settings while others in the group record the speaker's key adjectives and expressions.

Before sending the groups off, Mr. Nelson refers them to an anchor chart from an earlier lesson he had taught on speaking with confidence. He briefly demonstrates how the characteristics on the chart will apply to their small-group discussions.

In one group, Juan sits up confidently. He looks group members in the eye, and speaks loud enough for them to hear but not so loud as to disturb nearby

Common Core Connections · · · · · · · 41

How to Teach the Skills:

Taking Turns · · · · · · · · · · · · · · · 45
Speaking Confidently · · · · · · · · · 50
Staying on Topic · · · · · · · · · · · 53
Speaking With Clarity · · · · · · · · 56

Giving Meaningful Feedback · · · · 61

Addressing Common Mistakes · · 63

Essential Skills at a Glance · · · · · · · 66

Sample Letter to Parents · · · · · · · · 67

groups. He says, "My story takes place at night in the woods. It's really dark, and there's only a little light from a small sliver of the moon. But there's just enough to make scary shadows."

He continues, "The trees are tall, and some of the branches look like big arms. The wind is howling and it feels really cold. There are crunchy leaves underfoot and gooey mud, too." Juan smiles and adds, "I could keep going, but basically, it's a creepy night."

Juan's groupmates smile, too, and then take turns telling him a few of the adjectives and descriptive details that stood out to them. Juan's ability to express his ideas effectively helped him prepare for writing his story and gave his group members a vision for how they in turn could describe their own story settings.

In this chapter, you'll learn why speaking skills like those Juan demonstrated are so important for every child. Then you'll get a road map for teaching students how to take turns in conversations, demonstrate confidence as they share ideas, stay on topic, and speak with clarity.

Why These Skills Matter

Essential speaking skills are critical because they:

→ **Help students exchange ideas with classmates.** For instance, students need solid speaking skills to clearly explain problem-solving strategies in math, express opinions in literature circles, give constructive feedback during writers' workshop, respectfully debate in social studies, and productively discuss science topics.

→ **Form the building blocks for higher-level speaking skills**, such as making persuasive arguments, defending one's position, asking thought-provoking questions and offering thoughtful answers, and agreeing or disagreeing with another speaker's ideas. (See Chapters 3–5 for an approach  to teaching these higher-level speaking skills.) Learning to speak with clarity and choosing precise words also strengthens students' critical thinking skills.

→ **Prepare students for more formal speaking situations**, such as making presentations or giving speeches.

→ **Support students' relationships with classmates and others.** As students learn to express their ideas and feelings more clearly and confidently, they'll be able to communicate better in their social relationships. And, in turn, their clear communication will lead to fewer misunderstandings and hurt feelings from miscommunication, whether in the classroom, on the playground, at lunch, or on the bus.

✳ Common Core Connections

Kindergarten	**SL.K.1:** Participate in collaborative conversations with diverse partners about kindergarten topics and texts. **SL.K.1a:** Follow agreed-upon rules for discussions (e.g., listening to others and taking turns speaking). **SL.K.4:** Describe familiar people, places, things, and events and, with prompting and support, provide additional detail. **SL.K.6:** Speak audibly.
1st Grade	**SL.1.1:** Participate in collaborative conversations with diverse partners about grade 1 topics and texts. **SL.1.1a:** Follow agreed-upon rules for discussions (e.g., listening to others with care, speaking one at a time). **SL.1.4:** Describe familiar people, places, things, and events with relevant details, expressing ideas and feelings clearly. **SL.1.6:** Produce complete sentences when appropriate to task and situation.
2nd Grade	**SL.2.1:** Participate in collaborative conversations with diverse partners about grade 2 topics and texts. **SL.2.1a:** Follow agreed-upon rules for discussions (e.g., gaining the floor in respectful ways, listening with care, speaking one at a time). **SL.2.2:** Recount or describe key ideas or details from a text read aloud or information presented orally or through other media. **SL.2.4:** Tell a story or recount an experience with appropriate facts and relevant, descriptive details, speaking audibly in coherent sentences. **SL.2.6:** Produce complete sentences when appropriate to task and situation in order to provide requested detail or clarification.

Speaking and Listening Standards Supported in Chapter Two

3rd Grade

SL.3.1: Engage effectively in a range of collaborative discussions (one-on-one, in groups, and teacher-led) with diverse partners on grade 3 topics and texts.

SL.3.1a: Come to discussions prepared.

SL.3.1b: Follow agreed-upon rules for discussions (e.g., gaining the floor in respectful ways, listening to others with care, speaking one at a time).

SL.3.4: Report on a topic or text, tell a story, or recount an experience with appropriate facts and relevant, descriptive details, speaking clearly at an understandable pace.

SL.3.6: Speak in complete sentences when appropriate to task and situation in order to provide requested detail or clarification.

4th Grade

SL.4.1: Engage effectively in a range of collaborative discussions (one-on-one, in groups, and teacher-led) with diverse partners on grade 4 topics and texts.

SL.4.1a: Come to discussions prepared.

SL.4.1b: Follow agreed-upon rules for discussions and carry out assigned roles.

SL.4.4: Report on a topic or text, tell a story, or recount an experience in an organized manner, using appropriate facts and relevant, descriptive details to support main ideas or themes; speak clearly at an understandable pace.

SL.4.6: Differentiate between contexts that call for formal English and situations where informal discourse is appropriate; use formal English when appropriate to task and situation.

Speaking and Listening Standards Supported in Chapter Two

5th Grade

SL.5.1: Engage effectively in a range of collaborative discussions (one-on-one, in groups, and teacher-led) with diverse partners on grade 5 topics and texts.

SL.5.1a: Come to discussions prepared.

SL.5.1b: Follow agreed-upon rules for discussions and carry out assigned roles.

SL.5.4: Report on a topic or text or present an opinion, sequencing ideas logically and using appropriate facts and relevant, descriptive details to support main ideas or themes; speak clearly at an understandable pace.

SL.5.6: Adapt speech to a variety of contexts and tasks, using formal English when appropriate to task and situation.

6th Grade

SL.6.1: Engage effectively in a range of collaborative discussions (one-on-one, in groups, and teacher-led) with diverse partners on grade 6 topics and texts.

SL.6.1a: Come to discussions prepared.

SL.6.1b: Follow rules for collegial discussions.

SL.6.4: Present claims and findings, sequencing ideas logically and using pertinent descriptions, facts, and details to accentuate main ideas or themes; use appropriate eye contact, adequate volume, and clear pronunciation.

SL.6.6: Adapt speech to a variety of contexts and tasks, demonstrating command of formal English when indicated or appropriate.

How to Teach the Skills

Four essential speaking skills

✔ **Taking turns**

✔ **Speaking confidently**

✔ **Staying on topic**

✔ **Speaking with clarity**

Here are some guidelines to help you teach students these essential skills:

→ **Be empathetic.** Many children—and adults—find public speaking challenging, even in small groups.

→ **Remember where children are developmentally.** For instance, younger children may struggle with waiting for a turn to speak and need more support to do so. Older students may become more self-conscious and struggle with eye contact, so they may do better in small groups at first.

→ **Keep in mind children's cultural backgrounds.** If you're teaching skills that might conflict with a child's home culture, such as making eye contact when speaking, remember to respectfully acknowledge the home culture and present these as skills that can support success in school, college, and the workplace.

→ **Teach skills progressively.** Begin with the most basic or essential skills and build toward greater complexity as children are ready.

→ **Choose engaging topics when teaching these skills and having students practice them.** This fosters active participation by every student. Also choose topics that are most likely to feel comfortable to every child.

→ **Weave the teaching of speaking skills into academic lessons.** Often you can teach basic speaking skills within your regularly planned academic lessons.

On the following pages, I offer practical ways to teach speaking skills in the natural course of the school day. These steps will help your students see and feel how each skill looks and sounds in action, and give them many chances to practice in a variety of academic contexts.

For a suggested timeline of when to teach academic conversation skills throughout the school year, see page 191.

TAKING TURNS

For any conversation, knowing when to speak—and when to listen—is essential. I begin teaching basic speaking skills on the first day of school by introducing how to take turns in the whole group. After all, it's very hard to do any other teaching until students know how to participate in whole-group discussions. Then, when students are ready, I move on to teaching the other speaking skills.

Taking Turns in a Whole Group

Introduce the skill. Interactive Modeling (page 172) is an especially effective technique for teaching students the basic skill of taking turns. On the first day of school, you can use Interactive Modeling to teach students:

➥ **When and how to raise their hands** (or use another designated turn-taking procedure). Open the lesson by highlighting why this procedure matters:

> "We all need to feel that we have an equal chance to speak and be heard. When you have something you want to say in a discussion, there's a certain way to respectfully show it. Watch how I do that."

After modeling (without narration), ask students what they noticed. Be sure students point out that you raised your hand high, held it still, and waited until called on to speak.

➥ **When and how to put your hand down.** For this modeling, have one student act the part of the teacher. You and another student act the part of students who both have your hands raised to speak. "The teacher" calls on that student. Model for the class what to do in this situation. Highlight how you put your hand down as soon as that student was called on so that you could give him your full attention.

For younger students, you may want to use a think-aloud technique to show that even though you felt disappointed that you didn't get a turn to speak, you still put your hand down calmly. When teaching first graders, I would hold up a paper thought-bubble on a craft stick and say:

"At first, I was sad that the teacher called on Giselle and not me. But then I reminded myself we have to take turns and I might get to talk soon."

Practice the skill. Throughout those first few days of school, give students many chances to practice taking turns. Make the most of this practice by:

→ **Being consistent.** Be sure students follow the procedures as you taught them. Letting students call out instead of signaling for a turn will confuse them and extend the time it takes them to learn these skills.

→ **Giving frequent and supportive feedback.** Give students positive feedback when you notice them following the procedures as you taught. Do the same for students who struggle with these skills but are making progress. Briefly and respectfully redirect students who aren't following the procedures. (See pages 61–65 for more suggestions.)

Provide ongoing support. Even though whole-group turn-taking procedures seem so basic, you may still need to provide extra support for some students. For instance:

→ **Have certain students sit closer to you** so that you can give them a nonverbal cue to take turns if they forget.

→ **Use an anchor chart** to remind students to keep listening even when they're disappointed because you called on someone else.

Taking Turns in the Whole Group

* Listen.

* Raise your hand to signal that you want to speak.

* Wait to be called on.

* Put your hand down calmly if someone else is chosen.

→ **Review expectations with students before beginning** a whole-group discussion. For instance, "Who can remind us how we take turns during a whole-group conversation?" or "Let's remember how we take care of each other during our discussions—hand up to speak, wait to be called on, and put your hand down calmly if you're not called on."

Taking Turns With a Partner

Introduce the skill. As soon as most students have mastered whole-group expectations, begin teaching them how to take turns with a partner. You can use Interactive Modeling (page 172) to show students how to:

→ **sit or stand during partner chats** (for instance, knee to knee when sitting)

→ **signal to their partner that it's his or her turn:**

> What do you think?

> I want to hear your ideas.

> Would you like to go first?

> OK, your turn.

→ **let their partner know they're finished speaking:**

> That's all for now.

> I'm finished for now.

> I have more to say, but I want to hear your ideas before we run out of time.

→ check in to make sure their partner is finished:

> Was that all you wanted to say?

> May I take my turn now?

> Did you have any other ideas?

You can do this teaching as a stand-alone modeling lesson or weave it into an academic lesson, just before asking students to work with a partner.

Practice the skill. Once you've taught partner skills, give students multiple and varied opportunities to practice them—discussing with a partner a book they're reading, word problems in math, and observations in science. To add the variety that will keep students engaged, use different practice structures for partner talks, such as Info Exchange and Inside-Outside Circles (pages 179–180).

Provide ongoing support. While students are still getting the hang of partner talks, post anchor charts of sentences to use, such as the ones on this and the previous page, to indicate they're finished speaking or to make sure their partner is finished. For younger students, give each partner a set of sentence starters to hold and use. If students have difficulty taking turns with a partner, use a kitchen timer or watch to set a time limit for each speaker.

Taking Turns in Small Groups

Introduce the skill. Once most students have mastered turn-taking in whole groups and with partners, begin teaching how to take turns in small groups. These skills are more challenging—when everyone in a small group wants to speak, it's harder to go back and forth among speakers and balance everyone's "air time."

These skills are best demonstrated multiple times and in different academic contexts. For example, right before students break into small groups to discuss a book they've been reading, do some initial teaching about how to take turns in the group. You can use the Fishbowl technique (page 174) to show students how to:

- ⇥ tell if someone is finished making a point

- ⇥ listen for a natural pause to interject

- ⇥ know how long to speak

- ⇥ decide when to be quiet and let others have a turn

Remember, before you do the Fishbowl, practice with your student modelers the turn-taking skills you want them to demonstrate. For the actual lesson, remind the class to note exactly how the modelers make sure that everyone has an equal chance to speak: "See what each member of the group does so that everyone has time to share ideas."

Practice the skill and provide ongoing support. Anchor charts can be especially helpful reminders as students learn how long they should speak and how to know when to stay quiet.

You may also want to use a talking stick to designate in a more visible way whose turn it is to speak. When a child finishes speaking, she passes the stick to another person, who then takes his turn to speak.

> ## Taking Turns in a Small Group
>
> * Be brief—make one or two points.
>
> * Listen as others speak.
>
> * Wait to add more until everyone else has had a turn to speak.

Or give each group an index card with a speech bubble on it. Students pass the card back and forth, depending on whose turn it is to talk.

Move to "natural" turn-taking when students are ready. Natural turn-taking—without anyone calling on speakers, or using talking sticks or index cards—allows conversations to really flow while ensuring that everyone has multiple chances to speak.

When your students are adept at structured turn-taking, have them try this more free-flowing way of speaking. (Students in grades K–2 may not be ready for natural turn-taking at all.) Structures such as Popcorn and 20 Questions (pages 182 and 185) are especially useful for this teaching.

SPEAKING CONFIDENTLY

In the opening story for this chapter, Juan was able to speak so confidently because his teacher had deliberately taught the class how. Rather than assuming that his students would be able to speak with confidence, this teacher thought about the specific skills that academic speaking requires, taught each one, and provided students with opportunities to practice and master them throughout the year.

Confident speaking is a critical skill because it helps speakers feel more sure of themselves and invites listeners to pay attention to what a speaker is saying. Much of communication is nonverbal, so when speakers nonverbally convey a sense of authority and confidence, listeners are more likely to trust what they have to say.

Crucial skills to teach are:

→ **having a confident body posture**—sitting up, turning toward the listener, and, for older students, keeping bodies still and avoiding distracting gestures

→ **making eye contact**—and when talking to more than one person, making "roving" eye contact

→ **speaking at an appropriate volume and pace**—younger students can learn the Goldilocks Principle: not too loud, not too soft, not too fast, not too slow; older students can begin to understand how to vary volume and pace to make their points more effectively

If your students have had prior experience in learning to speak confidently, you could teach these skills in one lesson. Otherwise, it may help to break the teaching into two parts—body posture and eye contact first and then volume and pace.

Body Posture and Eye Contact

Introduce the skills. You can use Interactive Modeling (page 172) to do this teaching, emphasizing why these skills matter:

> "Everyone in this class has important contributions to make to our conversations. I'm going to show you one way to encourage classmates to take what you say seriously. Watch how I use my face and body when I share an observation about our science experiment."

Be sure to model and have students point out each key aspect—having an upright body posture, turning toward the listeners, and making eye contact with them.

Practice the skills. Give students multiple opportunities to practice using appropriate body language and eye contact in whole-group, partner, and small-group conversations. For example, have students:

⇢ **share a simple piece of personal information** (for instance, a sport they love and why) with the whole class during morning meeting

⇢ **explain to a small group** during readers' workshop how they used a particular decoding strategy

⇢ **turn and talk with a partner** about how they solved a math problem

Guide students to reflect frequently on how they're doing with body posture and eye contact, asking them to highlight which aspects are coming easily to them and which are still a challenge.

Provide ongoing support. You can use a simple anchor chart (like the one shown) to remind students of the key aspects you modeled.

Refer to this chart as you send students off to have conversations in various subjects. For example, before having students turn and talk with a partner about what vocabulary they found particularly challenging in a given text, you might say:

> We speak with confidence by:
> * Sitting up straight
> * Looking at listeners
> * Speaking loud enough to be heard

> "Who can remind us of how we can speak with confidence to help our partner understand us?"

Remember also to give positive feedback when students put these skills to use. For example, after partners share, you might say:

> "I saw many people with bodies still and shoulders back, and looking partners in the eye. You're really learning what confident speech looks like!"

Volume and Pace

Introduce the skills. You can do this in connection with an academic lesson that has students working in pairs. For instance, after students have read an intriguing text in social studies, have them discuss with a partner the most important facts and any questions they still have.

But before sending students off for their partner chats, use the Fishbowl technique (page 174) to teach them how to vary their volume and pace to match the substance of what they're saying. (Remember to prepare the student modelers in advance.) To introduce this quick demonstration, you might say:

> "People are more likely to listen and be interested in what you have to say if you use your voice to show how you're feeling about your ideas. Watch how the speakers in our Fishbowl today talk faster or slower, more quietly or more loudly, depending on what they're saying."

Guide students in pointing out that the speakers did things such as slowing their pace when posing an intriguing question, raising their volume slightly to show strong belief in an opinion, or keeping their volume and pace even-keeled to show matter-of-factness about a certain point.

Practice the skills and provide ongoing support. Once you've taught students how to vary their volume and pace, give them plenty of opportunities to practice. For example, here's how to use Say Something (page 184) for this practice:

→ **Give pairs of students a thought-provoking reading passage** (divided into chunks) about a current event.

→ **After reading each chunk, partners take turns "saying something"** (one sentence) about what they read (something they questioned, found interesting, or want to know more about), being especially conscious of how they use their voices—volume and pacing—to convey meaning.

→ **Remind students that their statements do not have to be related,** and they should not respond to each other specifically. Once partners finish the entire passage, they may engage in open conversation about it and respond to their partner's earlier comments or questions.

→ **Debrief as a class** about how they used pacing and volume to make their points.

STAYING ON TOPIC

Most students find it challenging to stay on topic, whether writing or speaking. Besides making sure all comments "stick" to the topic at hand, this skill set includes self-correcting (if veering off topic) and knowing when to respectfully pass or stop (if there's nothing new to add).

This skill set requires considerable judgment and nuance, so begin simply and add complexity as students are ready.

Essentials of Staying on Topic

Introduce the skill. Staying on topic requires several layers of understanding—clearly knowing what the topic is, thinking of ideas that are relevant to that topic, and discarding any ideas that are irrelevant, even ones that might be interesting. Here are two ways to intoduce the essentials of staying on topic—one for older students and one for younger students:

> ➙ **For older students,** a Focused Brainstorm (page 176) works well. In Mr. Lopez's fourth grade class, students are about to go into literature circles to discuss the book they read yesterday, *Those Shoes* by Maribeth Boelts. Mr. Lopez first takes a moment to prepare students to stay on topic in their discussions:

> "Suppose Zari starts and says, 'I didn't understand what the grandmother meant when she said *There's no room for want around here, just need.*' In conversations, we want to stay on topic. So what are some comments we could make that would help keep the learning going and stay on the topic Zari raised? Chat with a neighbor about some ideas."

After a minute, Mr. Lopez asks students to share their ideas:

> **We can try to figure it out together using other clues in the text.**

> **We could just say what we think that means.**

> **We can say, "I didn't understand, either. Maybe we should look up some words in the dictionary."**

When a student suggests they could "talk about things we want to have," Mr. Lopez points out that this idea, while interesting, relates to a different topic: "Let's save that for later when we're making personal connections to the story."

→ **With younger students,** I've taught these skills using an Expert Demonstration (page 175). I invite a small group of fifth grade students to demonstrate to first graders how to stay on topic, using a subject easily accessible to first graders, such as an animal habitat they're studying.

Before the demonstration, I tell the first graders that the topic of conversation is "what we observed about the habitat" and alert them to notice how the fifth graders keep their comments focused on that topic.

After the demonstration, I invite the first graders to share some of the comments they heard and then I let them know why those comments stayed on topic. For instance, a first grader might note that one of the fifth graders said that the millipedes in the classroom terrarium had already made lots of holes in the dirt. I might follow up and say, "He was describing exactly what he saw—that's just what I asked his group to do."

If the demonstrators make comments that the first graders aren't sure were on topic, I use these as a teaching opportunity to explore in more depth what "on topic" means. For instance, if a fifth grader said, "I think millipedes are really cool," I might follow up by saying, "That would be a great thing to talk about later, but it wasn't on topic because it didn't describe specifically what she saw about the millipedes' habitat."

Practice the skill and provide ongoing support. Because staying on topic is such a challenging skill, provide support as students practice.

→ **Give "rehearsal" time.** For example, have students brainstorm brief, on-topic answers or comments with a partner first. Then open the discussion up for students to share with the whole class what they brainstormed.

→ **Give students relatively straightforward topics** at first; then add more open-ended and complex ones.

→ **Keep the time for discussions brief** at first so that students encounter success with staying on topic. The longer students talk, the easier it is for them to get sidetracked in their thinking or run out of on-topic ideas.

→ **Teach students how to help each other out** if they get off track. Show them a respectful signal to use when they notice someone is straying from the topic.

→ **Use practice structures** such as Say Something and Swap Meet (page 184) to give students additional practice in staying on topic with partners and in small groups.

Self-Correcting and Respectfully Passing

After introducing and practicing the skill of staying on topic, you can use Interactive Modeling (page 172) to teach students how to self-correct, if they notice they have strayed from the topic, and how to respectfully pass or stop, if they have nothing new to add. Highlight why these skills matter:

→ **Self-correcting.** "Sometimes in conversations we lose track of where we are or stray off topic. That's OK—it happens to everyone. When that happens, there are some words we can use to get back on track and show our listeners what happened. Watch how I use one of those statements."

"I'm sorry. I need to get back to the question we were discussing."

"But, to return to what we were talking about . . ."

"Oops, I think I've gotten off track."

Provide anchor charts (like the one shown) for students to use for additional support.

→ **Respectfully passing.** "It's important to know how to contribute your ideas during a group discussion, but it's just as important to know when to be silent if you have nothing new to add. Watch how I do that in a way that is respectful and quick." When you model, use a straightforward sentence and an even tone. For example: "I will pass for now." Be sure students notice that you spoke briefly and showed with your face and voice that you were still interested in the topic and respectful of what others had to say.

Remember to positively comment when you see students using these skills. For example, if you observe a student during a partner discussion specifically note that she was getting off track, you might say:

> "J.C., I noticed that when you went off on a tangent, you realized it quickly and apologized to Teddy. That took care of both of you and helped you keep on learning."

SPEAKING WITH CLARITY

To successfully engage in academic conversations, students need to clarify ideas in their own minds first and then know how to express those ideas clearly to others. Key skills for them to learn are:

→ **pausing before speaking** to organize thoughts

→ **speaking in complete sentences** when appropriate

→ **choosing precise words** and being as specific as possible

Pausing Before Speaking

Introduce the skill. Pausing to gather one's thoughts not only raises the quality of students' conversations, it's also essential for their success with writing and test-taking. You can use an Interactive Modeling lesson (page 172) to teach this skill. Start by letting students know why pausing before speaking will help them:

> "Our conversations will be more thoughtful and interesting if we all stop and briefly think about what we want to say before we speak. I'm going to show you how this looks. Watch and see what you notice I do when it's my turn."

After showing students what pausing looks like, use a think-aloud technique to show them what you were doing as you paused. Point to your head and say,

"When I paused, I was thinking that I wanted to share my prediction about what might happen in our science experiment first and give my reason second. Then, I quickly thought of the actual words I would use."

Use tangible reminders as students practice. Some examples are:

⇢ **A thought-bubble.** You might hold up a paper thought-bubble to remind a student to think before speaking.

⇢ **A digital timer.** Reset it each time a classmate finishes speaking. Students wait until time is up before speaking.

⇢ **A teacher signal.** Let students know that they should pause and think until you give the signal to speak.

Provide additional support as needed. For younger students, I also use Interactive Modeling to show them how to help each other remember to pause during partner chats and small-group discussions. I also post some student language they can use like the ones shown here.

Older students may enjoy doing a Focused Brainstorm (page 176) to come up with their own words for helping their partners remember to pause.

Using Complete Sentences

Introduce the skill. After students learn to pause, I teach them how to use complete sentences to communicate effectively. Although complete sentences aren't necessary

"We should remember to wait a few seconds before speaking."

"Let's stop first and think about what we're going to say."

"We should pause first and then speak."

all the time, they are important for academic conversations to be thorough and rich, and they help students to think more clearly and completely. Because using complete sentences is such a critical skill, I try to teach and reinforce it throughout the school day, every day, and across all subject areas.

→ **For all students,** you can use Interactive Modeling (page 172) to introduce the skill and explain why it matters. You might say, "When we're discussing topics at school—whether in reading, math, social studies, or science—we want to be as clear as possible. One way to do that is to speak in complete sentences. Watch and see how this looks and sounds as I discuss how I sorted shapes in math." Guide students to identify your complete sentences and how each helped you make your point clearly.

→ **For older students,** I sometimes use a Focused Brainstorm (page 176) for this teaching. You can provide students with a prompt, such as what they think is going to happen next in a read-aloud. Then have them brainstorm possiblities and say them using complete sentences. Record their sentences and, after briefly discussing the content of their responses, analyze their sentence constructions as a group using open-ended questions, such as "Why are these complete sentences? What different sentence constructions did people use?"

Give students multiple ways to practice. You can have students practice complete sentences whenever they're engaged in academic conversations. Here are some ideas to ensure rich conversations that hold students' interest:

→ **Swap Meet**—Pose an open-ended question to the class, such as "What evidence can you find in this chapter to support the author's conclusion that insects can be helpful to humans? Review the chapter and list your ideas." Direct students to find a partner and swap one idea in a complete sentence. Students then find another partner and repeat the process. Continue for a few more rounds.

→ **Inside-Outside Circles**—Give students topics to discuss and have them talk with one partner at a time, using complete sentences. For example, when studying the characteristics of certain shapes in math, you might present a block, name one shape, and have each partner discuss in complete sentences whether the block meets the characteristics of that shape and explain why or why not. Then have students take a step to the right so everyone has a new partner. Name a new shape for partners to discuss. Repeat for several shapes.

⇢ **Maître d'**—Have students quickly form small groups and use complete sentences to discuss a topic. For example, you might pose a statement about a character in a book the class has been reading and have groups come up with specific examples from the text to support or refute that statement. Then have students quickly form new groups and pose a different statement. Repeat a few times.

For more on these techniques, see pages 180–184.

Support students by giving them sentence starters. To help guide students in consistently using complete sentences, provide sentence starters (or the sentence structure to be used). For example: "I believe the answer is going to be more than _____ because I figured out that _____."

Choosing Precise Words and Being Specific

Introduce the skills. Once students have made progress with pausing before speaking and using complete sentences, begin encouraging them to think about their word choice. Some tools for this teaching include:

⇢ **Focused Brainstorm**—Give students time to study an object related to their unit of study, such as a three-dimensional figure, bird's nest, or painting, and then have them brainstorm words to describe it. Next, lead them in sorting the words according to whether they were general (and could describe many things) or specific and descriptive of the object. For instance, if students observed a bird's next, the sorting might look like this:

General	Specific and Descriptive
Cool	Brown
Pretty	Has sticks
Interesting	Small
	Indented in center

This lesson supports students' development of essential observation skills, so it could easily be included as part of a substantive lesson in math, science, or art.

→ **Fishbowl or Expert Demonstration—** Have a small group of students or experts model a brief conversation requiring precise vocabulary. For instance, students in the Fishbowl could describe what happened during a given historical event, a scene from a fiction or nonfiction text, or a science experiment. Prompt observers to listen closely for the language the speakers use and note particularly effective words.

See pages 174–176 for more on these techniques.

Support students as they practice. As students learn to be specific and descriptive with their language, consider having them:

→ **Work in pairs** to brainstorm words to use. For instance, before opening up a whole-group conversation in which students are going to share their results from a science experiment, have them turn to a partner and practice what they'll say, especially how they'll be precise in their descriptions of what happened.

→ **Post word webs or other graphic organizers** of key vocabulary related to a given lesson. For instance, if students are going to be comparing what they learned about different plants, post a graphic organizer with relevant words, such as the names of plant parts and the function of each.

Giving Meaningful Feedback

Students often need a great deal of encouragement to develop their academic speaking skills. They need to hear what they're doing well—and when they make mistakes, they need supportive, noncritical feedback.

BE SPECIFIC

By being specific, you can paint a picture for students of what they said, how they said it, and what they should do again in future conversations.

➜ Begin with "I saw" or "I heard" and name the important details you observed:

> "I saw you sitting up straight and moving your eyes around the circle as we practiced."

> "I heard people projecting their voices and using complete sentences so that everyone could hear and fully understand."

➜ Use an anchor chart as a starting point for specific feedback. Talk about how students did at each item on the chart.

> "Let's look at our chart and see what you did well. You spoke in complete sentences, which makes it easier to follow what you're saying. Everyone spoke at least once, so you shared air time equally."

REINFORCE POSITIVES OFTEN

When you see the whole class working successfully—for instance, staying on topic—tell them that you noticed. For example:

→ **If a small group makes sure** everyone has equal chances to speak, point out how they did that.

→ **If an individual speaks with confidence** and an appropriate volume, let her know (privately).

You cannot overdo positive reinforcing language. Such frequent positive feedback is especially powerful for shy or reluctant speakers.

GIVE UNQUALIFIED POSITIVE FEEDBACK

Students may minimize or discount positive feedback if it's immediately followed by a criticism. If students successfully apply many of the speaking skills you've been teaching, point out that success immediately without qualifying it.

Instead of . . .	Try . . .
"You remembered to raise your hands and make eye contact, but you were all speaking too quietly. I could barely hear some of you."	"You remembered to raise your hands and make eye contact. That's hard to do, and it's one of the most important ways to connect with listeners."
"I heard everyone staying on topic, but your body language could use improvement."	"I heard everyone staying on topic, discussing the theme. What you said made it easy for us to get to know the books you read, even though we didn't all read the same ones!"

To *yourself*, note the skill that was not as successful. Make that the focus of your next teaching.

Addressing Common Mistakes

When students make mistakes, try to tread lightly or they may become nervous about "messing up" the next time they speak. In the moment, get students back on track calmly and without judgment. Later, provide further teaching or practice if you sense they need it.

Tips for Addressing Mistakes

✔ **Correct mistakes** respectfully, with an encouraging tone.

✔ **Tell students how** to correct the mistake—and give them a chance to do it.

✔ **Set up nonverbal signals** ahead of time as reminders of expectations.

✔ **Be brief and to the point** to keep the conversation going.

SPEAKING TOO QUIETLY OR TENTATIVELY

Some children seem to shrink in the spotlight, even those who are boisterous at recess or lunch. They may get very quiet, sit with slumped shoulders, or look down at their laps. If this happens:

→ **Briefly remind the child of expectations.** Then give her a chance for a do-over.

> "Ava, eyes up and voice on. Say that important statement again."

> "Look at the anchor chart. Think about how we practiced projecting our voices."

→ **Respond nonverbally or privately, if possible.** Although feedback is most powerful when given in the moment, some students might be too embarrassed if you correct their mistakes publicly. If you sense this possibility, wait to give feedback privately as soon as possible after the event.

SPEAKING TOO MUCH

Some children have a hard time being succinct or want to contribute to the conversation multiple times. If students are speaking too much either way, try these techniques:

→ **Teach how to be succinct.** Show students how to make just one point at a time and to include only the key details. Interactive Modeling, Fishbowl, and Expert Demonstrations (pages 172–175) are useful techniques for this teaching.

→ **Set up nonverbal signals ahead of time.** For instance, once you have taught students to include only key details, agree on a respectful nonverbal reminder (such as holding up one finger) that you'll use when they go over this limit.

→ **Stop the student respectfully.** Hold students accountable for speaking succinctly and sharing the floor, but do so in a way that presumes their overparticipation arises from enthusiasm, not from a desire to take the focus away from others:

> "Noah, hand down for now. I'll come back to you in a few minutes."

> "Morgan, stop right there. That's enough detail. We need to hear from Emery and Jason before our time is up."

> "Elyse, pause for a second. The other members of your group need a turn now. Then you can make another point."

→ **Provide other outlets.** Some children may benefit from having additional opportunities to share ideas. You might arrange to have a private conference with those children or give them a notebook in which they can share more ideas with you. Then, in the moment, refer to those opportunities:

> "Joshua, you have made your three contributions. Wait and tell me the rest later during our conference time."

GOING OFF ON A TANGENT

Many children have a hard time staying on topic. One thought leads to another and before long, they have strayed far from the topic. If this happens, try to:

- ⇢ **Redirect nonjudgmentally.** A simple reminder delivered respectfully may be all they need to get back on track. For instance:

> "Hold on, Carly. We're just talking about whales right now. Make one more comment to share what you learned about them from your reading."

- ⇢ **Avoid asking questions.** Questions such as "What are you supposed to be talking about now?" may feel sarcastic and shut students down. It's more respectful and direct to tell students what to do in a kind and supportive tone.

> "Let's stay focused on our predictions about what will happen next in the story."

GRAMMAR MIX-UPS

Students often struggle with grammar as they speak. For instance, they might slip up with pronouns ("Me and Joshua thought . . .") or use a double negative construction ("Nobody hasn't ever discovered . . ."). When such missteps occur:

- ⇢ **Keep your focus on the content of what the student is saying.** Publicly correcting grammar may embarrass the speaker and discourage her from speaking in the future. Let the error go if the meaning is clear, and make a mental note to work on grammar later, privately or with the whole class.

- ⇢ **Try paraphrasing or checking in, using correct grammar.** If you suspect that other listeners may not understand the speaker's meaning due to the grammatical mistake, you may want to check in with the speaker. When you do so, model correct grammar usage.

> "So are you saying that no one has discovered what is causing bees to die off?"

Essential Skills at a Glance

SPEAKING	
Taking Turns (pages 45–49)	⇢ Follow teacher-designated procedures for taking turns. —in a whole group —with a partner —in a small group
Speaking Confidently (pages 50–52)	⇢ Have a confident body posture. ⇢ Make eye contact. Make "roving" eye contact when speaking to more than one person. ⇢ Speak at an appropriate volume and pace.
Staying on Topic (pages 53–56)	⇢ Make sure all comments are relevant to the topic. ⇢ Self-correct if starting to veer away from the topic. ⇢ Stop or respectfully pass if you have nothing new to add.
Speaking With Clarity (pages 56–60)	⇢ Pause before thinking to plan what to say. ⇢ Speak in complete sentences. ⇢ Choose precise words and be as specific as possible.

Sample Letter to Parents

Dear Parents,

This week, we began working on the skills required for speaking with confidence—sitting up straight, making eye contact, and speaking at an appropriate volume. These skills are important not just for conversations at school but for all sorts of situations your child will encounter outside of school.

If you want to help your child practice these skills, here are a few simple ways to do so:

- Encourage your child to make a request, place an order, or thank customer service workers at stores and restaurants by using skills for confident speaking.

- Help your child remember to speak with confidence when talking with grandparents, neighbors, or other adults.

- Share with your child how you try to use these skills yourself at work, when volunteering, or in new social situations.

- Reinforce your child's efforts. For instance, comment positively when you notice him or her trying to speak with confidence.

If you have any questions, please contact me. Thank you for supporting your child's learning!

Asking and Answering Questions

Curious, Relevant, Purposeful

Curiosity is at the heart of learning—and a healthy curiosity depends on questioning. Learning to ask and answer questions moves children beyond themselves; they become able not only to consider what they know or think but to seek out the knowledge and opinions of others. To do this, children need to know how to ask relevant, respectful, and probing questions and how to answer questions thoughtfully and succinctly.

In one sixth grade classroom, students use their questioning skills to push their own thinking as well as that of their classmate Patrick, who's sharing the results of his science experiment. Patrick explains that he was researching different methods of softening avocados. He placed one avocado in a refrigerator, one in a plastic bag, one in a paper bag, and one in a paper bag with a banana. The latter softened the fastest. As he finishes sharing, his classmates show their enthusiasm and interest through their questions in the ensuing discussion: "How did you decide on those four methods?"

Common Core Connections · · · · · · · 71

How to Teach the Skills:

Question or Statement? · · · · · · · · 75
Asking Questions Respectfully · · 77
Asking Purposeful Questions · · · 79
Giving High-Quality Answers · · · · 85

Giving Meaningful Feedback · · · · 92

Addressing Common Mistakes · · · 95

Essential Skills at a Glance · · · · · · · 97

Sample Letter to Parents · · · · · · · · 98

"How long did you leave them?" "Did any of them not get soft at all?" "Why did the banana make such a difference?" "What would you want to find out about avocados next?"

Patrick answers several questions, demonstrating the depth of his insights into his research. But, as he tries to answer other questions, he also realizes that he has more work to do. He thanks the group and lets them know he'll get back to them after more research.

The probing questions his classmates asked helped them connect to Patrick's work and deepened everyone's understanding of science. They also helped those still conducting their own experiments to consider similar issues about their work— and they helped Patrick think about his experiment in new ways.

In this chapter, you'll learn about the why's and how's of teaching questioning skills so that students can learn to think and probe in the same deep ways that Patrick and his classmates did. You'll also learn how to teach students to answer questions clearly and concisely.

Why These Skills Matter

Knowing how to ask and answer questions effectively is essential to classroom conversations—and to children's becoming life-long learners. Question and answer skills:

→ **Foster curiosity and engagement.** All new inventions, innovations, discoveries, and true learning started with someone's curiosity. Children, who naturally thirst for knowledge, will learn more and do so at a deeper level if they know how to ask and answer questions.

→ **Lead to deeper, richer conversations.** Questions allow students to move beyond simply understanding what another person said to being able to actively engage with the meaning and significance of his content. Although students can learn a great deal by exchanging ideas, effective questions move both the speaker and the listener to new and deeper levels of understanding.

→ **Support children's academic growth across subject areas.** The more practice students have in using question and answer skills, the more prepared they'll be to think critically when they read, explore science concepts, investigate historical events, and solve math problems. These skills are also critical for students' success on standardized tests.

→ **Boost children's ability to communicate with others socially.** Learning to ask appropriate questions will help children develop empathy for their friends, classmates, and family members, and knowing how to answer questions will help them deepen their social conversations and relationships with others as well. Stronger social relationships in turn will lead to happier emotional lives and more effective learning communities.

✳ Common Core Connections

Kindergarten	**SL.K.1:** Participate in collaborative conversations with diverse partners about kindergarten topics and texts.

SL.K.1a: Follow agreed-upon rules for discussions (e.g., listening to others and taking turns speaking).

SL.K.2: Confirm understanding of a text read aloud or information presented orally or through other media by asking and answering questions about key details and requesting clarification if something is not understood.

SL.K.3: Ask and answer questions in order to seek help, get information, or clarify something that is not understood.

SL.K.6: Speak audibly and express thoughts, feelings, and ideas clearly. |
| **1st Grade** | **SL.1.1:** Participate in collaborative conversations with diverse partners about grade 1 topics and texts.

SL.1.1a: Follow agreed-upon rules for discussions (e.g., listening to others with care, speaking one at a time).

SL.1.1c: Ask questions to clear up any confusion about the topics and texts under discussion.

SL.1.2: Ask and answer questions about key details in a text read aloud or information presented orally or through other media.

SL.1.3: Ask and answer questions about what a speaker says in order to gather additional information or clarify something that is not understood.

SL.1.6: Produce complete sentences when appropriate to task and situation. |

	Speaking and Listening Standards Supported in Chapter Three
2nd Grade	**SL.2.1:** Participate in collaborative conversations with diverse partners about grade 2 topics and texts.
	SL.2.1a: Follow agreed-upon rules for discussions (e.g., gaining the floor in respectful ways, listening with care, speaking one at a time).
	SL.2.2: Recount or describe key ideas or details from a text read aloud or information presented orally or through other media.
	SL.2.4: Tell a story or recount an experience with appropriate facts and relevant, descriptive details, speaking audibly in coherent sentences.
	SL.2.6: Produce complete sentences when appropriate to task and situation in order to provide requested detail or clarification.
3rd Grade	**SL.3.1:** Engage effectively in a range of collaborative discussions (one-on-one, in groups, and teacher-led) with diverse partners on grade 3 topics and texts.
	SL.3.1a: Come to discussions prepared.
	SL.3.1b: Follow agreed-upon rules for discussions (e.g., gaining the floor in respectful ways, listening to others with care, speaking one at a time).
	SL.3.4: Report on a topic or text, tell a story, or recount an experience with appropriate facts and relevant, descriptive details, speaking clearly at an understandable pace.
	SL.3.6: Speak in complete sentences when appropriate to task and situation in order to provide requested detail or clarification.
4th Grade	**SL.4.1:** Engage effectively in a range of collaborative discussions (one-on-one, in groups, and teacher-led) with diverse partners on grade 4 topics and texts.
	SL.4.1a: Come to discussions prepared.
	SL.4.1b: Follow agreed-upon rules for discussions and carry out assigned roles.

4th Grade, cont.	**SL.4.4:** Report on a topic or text, tell a story, or recount an experience in an organized manner, using appropriate facts and relevant, descriptive details to support main ideas or themes; speak clearly at an understandable pace. **SL.4.6:** Differentiate between contexts that call for formal English and situations where informal discourse is appropriate; use formal English when appropriate to task and situation.
5th Grade	**SL.5.1:** Engage effectively in a range of collaborative discussions (one-on-one, in groups, and teacher-led) with diverse partners on grade 5 topics and texts. **SL.5.1a:** Come to discussions prepared. **SL.5.1b:** Follow agreed-upon rules for discussions and carry out assigned roles. **SL.5.4:** Report on a topic or text or present an opinion, sequencing ideas logically and using appropriate facts and relevant, descriptive details to support main ideas or themes; speak clearly at an understandable pace. **SL.5.6:** Adapt speech to a variety of contexts and tasks, using formal English when appropriate to task and situation.
6th Grade	**SL.6.1:** Engage effectively in a range of collaborative discussions (one-on-one, in groups, and teacher-led) with diverse partners on grade 6 topics and texts. **SL.6.1a:** Come to discussions prepared. **SL.6.1b:** Follow rules for collegial discussions. **SL.6.4:** Present claims and findings, sequencing ideas logically and using pertinent descriptions, facts, and details to accentuate main ideas or themes; use appropriate eye contact, adequate volume, and clear pronunciation. **SL.6.6:** Adapt speech to a variety of contexts and tasks, demonstrating command of formal English when indicated or appropriate.

How to Teach the Skills

Here are some guidelines for teaching students question and answer skills:

→ **Create an environment where questions are encouraged.** To foster students' curiosity, try to welcome questions, even if they're asked at inconvenient times or you can't answer them: "Why doesn't our clock have a second hand?" "How come our carpet is this color?" Encourage students to explore answers to their own questions whenever possible. Model what being inquisitive looks and sounds like—wonder aloud in front of your students.

→ **Start simply and gradually add in complexity.** Begin with the basics of asking questions—what a question is, how it sounds, and what vocabulary we use to ask questions. Then, as students get these essentials down, add the next skill until they're using questions at a high level.

→ **Use thought-provoking topics.** Children are more likely to ask interesting questions and be engaged in trying to answer questions when their curiosity is sparked and they can wrestle with challenging, interesting, or unusual content.

→ **Weave the teaching of questions into academics.** Because the skills in this chapter carry over into all academic areas, you can teach them and have children practice them as a natural part of academic lessons.

Essential skills for asking and answering questions

✔ **Question or statement?**

✔ **Asking questions respectfully**

✔ **Asking purposeful questions**

✔ **Giving high-quality answers**

→ **Consider students' developmental needs.** Although children are naturally curious, asking and answering questions effectively in the school setting can be tricky. For example, younger students may struggle with distinguishing between questions and statements. Older students may need encouragement to ask questions because they often worry about their social status and may not want to risk asking a "dumb" question or showing interest in an academic topic.

→ **Keep in mind children's cultural backgrounds.** If you're teaching skills that might conflict with a child's home culture, such as asking probing questions, remember to present these skills as ones that can support success in school, college, and the workplace.

As you teach question and answer skills, you'll want to give students a vision of why they matter, model exactly what it looks like and sounds like to use a particular skill, and offer many opportunities to practice these skills throughout the school day in all subject areas.

For a suggested timeline of when to teach academic conversation skills throughout the school year, see page 191.

QUESTION OR STATEMENT?

Although knowing the difference between a question and a statement may seem basic, some students, especially younger ones, may struggle with this distinction.

Introduce the skill. To ask questions, students first need to understand what a question is and how questions look and sound in academic conversations. You can use Interactive Modeling (page 172) to teach these basics so that students have a common foundation on which to build all further questioning skills. Here's a brief outline of how this lesson might look:

→ **State why knowing the difference between questions and statements matters.** Use an anchor chart like the one shown here to help make this distinction concrete.

Statements: TELL	Questions: ASK
I have a dog, too.	What kind of dog is it?
Your birthday sounds like it was fun.	How was your birthday?
Your book sounds exciting.	What do you think will happen next?

→ **Model asking simple questions.** Ask a student to share briefly about a book she just read. Then respond with a few questions. You may also want to use a variety of question words (see page 79) and point these out to students.

→ **Be sure students notice key aspects of the questioning.** Prompt students if they don't mention how your questions asked for something (for example, more information or clarification).

→ **Switch roles.** Share about something you've read, and then invite a student to ask you questions.

→ **Have students practice with partners.** Circulate and reinforce students' efforts.

Practice and provide support as needed:

→ **Guide students in sorting sentences** into questions or statements.

→ **Pose a question challenge.** At the end of a read-aloud chapter, challenge students to see how many different questions they can ask.

→ **Use practice structures** such as Inside-Outside Circles (page 180) for additional practice asking questions with partners and in small groups.

→ **Use morning meetings.** Invite students to share personal news and then take a few questions from classmates.

→ **Practice intonation** with students who need it. Some students use a questioning intonation when making statements. Work with these children in small groups or individually so they can learn to make statements that don't sound like questions.

ASKING QUESTIONS RESPECTFULLY

Introduce the skill. After students gain some competence with asking questions, teach them the importance of asking them respectfully. Students need to understand that respectful questions focus on what a speaker said, and are asked with genuine curiosity and friendly body language.

You can introduce respectful questioning by using the Fishbowl or Expert Demonstration techniques (pages 174–175). For instance, here's how one fourth grade teacher, Mr. Suarez, used the Fishbowl to introduce the concept of respectful questioning during a math lesson:

↪ **Set the purpose for the lesson.** After preparing the demonstrators in advance, Mr. Suarez began the Fishbowl by reminding the class how using questions had been leading to richer classroom conversations. He then said:

> "Today, we're going to go deeper by learning how to ask respectful questions—ones that focus on the speaker's ideas and show true interest in them. Watch how those in the Fishbowl do this after hearing what Sean has to say."

↪ **Choose an engaging topic for the demonstration.** Mr. Suarez had demonstrators discuss a survey about the class's TV watching. Sean began by briefly summarizing the results of the data he had collected and shared a graph he made during math class. The group then paused to think before asking questions:

Do you think your results are accurate?

If you had it to do over again, would you ask the same questions?

Did any results surprise or confuse you?

→ **Discuss the demonstration as a whole group.** Afterward, Mr. Suarez asked the class what they noticed about the questions the demonstrators asked. He listed their observations on the whiteboard.

How the questions showed respect for the speaker:

The askers wanted to know more about Sean's research. They didn't ask just for the sake of asking or to show what they themselves knew.

The askers didn't already know the answers to their questions.

Their faces and tone showed they were interested in Sean's ideas.

Mr. Suarez followed up by asking the class, "How did Lucius ask that question about the accuracy of Sean's results without sounding insulting?" Students noted that Lucius's tone of voice sounded friendly and curious, and showed that he didn't know the answer yet himself.

Practice the skill. Once students have a basic understanding of asking respectful questions, give them meaningful chances to practice.

→ **Play a round of Maître d'** (page 180) so students can discuss in small groups a challenging passage from a book the class is reading. Encourage them to place special emphasis on respectful questions.

> "Remember to ask questions with real curiosity and in a friendly way."

→ **Have students practice with partners.** Place students in pairs to brainstorm and list questions that they might ask after reading a certain passage, hearing a presentation, or listening to a classmate explain her thinking in math. Then have them cross out any questions that seem off topic, more about the asker, or not really seeking information because the asker already knows the answer. Finally, have partners practice the questions that remain, using a respectful, friendly tone.

Provide ongoing support.

⤳ **Post an anchor chart.** If you know that being respectful will be challenging for students, use an anchor chart to remind them of the key aspects of respectful questioning.

> **Questions are respectful if:**
> * You are curious about the answer.
> * You are not just trying to show what you know.
> * Your tone is kind.
> * Your face is friendly.

⤳ **Ask students to reflect on how they're doing with respectful questioning.** Children will have the best sense of whether questions feel respectful or not, so check in with them occasionally. For instance, after students share research projects and take questions about their findings, have them reflect: "On a scale of one to five, how respectful did the questions feel?"

ASKING PURPOSEFUL QUESTIONS

As your students become adept at asking respectful questions, the next step is to help them be truly purposeful with their questions. To deepen their thinking, students need to know how to ask specific questions for specific purposes, such as to get more background, seek someone's opinion, or get further clarification or explanation.

Recognizing and Using Question Words

> **Question Words**
> * Who * When * What
> * Why * Where * How

Introduce the skill. You can use the Fishbowl technique (page 174) to teach question words and show how using them will help students in all areas of their learning. If your students are not ready to demonstrate for the Fishbowl lesson, use Expert Demonstrators (page 175) who have more experience using question words. Here's how to do a Fishbowl lesson:

→ **Introduce the question words and state the purpose for the lesson.** After preparing in advance the demonstrators who will be in the Fishbowl, introduce the lesson:

> "On this chart, I've listed question starter words. The people in our Fishbowl are going to demonstrate how to use these words to ask purposeful questions about our science reading. Pay attention to how they use the question words and how these words help them understand each other better."

→ **Have students demonstrate for a few minutes.** One student in the Fishbowl summarizes what she read in the science text. After her summary, the others in the Fishbowl ask questions, using all the question words listed on the chart.

→ **Invite the class to share what they noticed.**

> "How did Keri, Jamel, and Vivica use question words to understand more about Tanya's summary on the discovery of electricity?"

→ **Have students do a quick practice.** Have pairs of students summarize another short text together and use as many question words as they can to improve their understanding of it.

Practice using the question words frequently. Here are some ideas to try:

→ **Use a "questions challenge."** Read aloud a brief, interesting excerpt from an informational text. Then, challenge students to work with a partner to see how many questions they can come up with using each of the question words. Next, have partners share one of their questions with the whole class. You might want to chart these questions for later use (for instance, in categorizing questions by purpose; see page 83).

→ **Have students conduct interviews.** Guide students in using the question words to interview classmates or family members about a specific event in their lives. This assignment helps students see how these question words enhance conversations and lead to deeper learning and personal connections.

→ **Practice through games.** For instance, students could play a variation of 20 Questions in science to explore the content they're studying (animals, for example) and use question words more purposefully.

- Tell the group you're thinking of an animal.

- Let them ask any kind of question, as long as it begins with one of the question words.

- The group can ask up to twenty questions to try to figure out what the animal is.

→ **Use KWL charts and similar structures.** The beginning of a new unit of study, research project, or read-aloud can present opportune times for asking questions. As you embark on a new math unit on fractions, for instance, you might ask students to reflect on what they already know about fractions and use the question words to explore what else they want to learn.

K: What We Think We Know	W: What We Want to Learn	L: What We Learned
Fractions have a top number and a bottom number. They are used for showing parts of something. They have a numerator and denominator.	What do people use them for? Why are they so hard to understand? How are they useful?	

When you use KWL charts, students may ask questions you had not planned to cover. If they do, you may want to assign them the questions to research and have them report back to the class. Then you could report all results, whether taught by you or reported by students, in the L (Learned) column.

Provide ongoing support. Asking questions using all the question words (not just some) may be harder than it seems, especially for students with limited experience cultivating their curiosity. Try these techniques to give students extra support:

→ **Have partners brainstorm.** Often students can think of more questions when working with a partner because one person's idea sparks another in her partner.

→ **Keep displaying question words and sample questions.** As you send students off to work or have discussions, remind them to put these displays to use.

> "As you discuss what you read in your literature circles today, refer to our question words chart. Afterward, we'll reflect on how many different questions you were able to ask each other."

→ **Paraphrase students' comments using question words.** For instance, a student might say, "I couldn't figure out what all that hair is doing on a bee's legs." You could rephrase for him by saying, "So a question you want to ask is 'Why do bees' legs have hair?'"

Being Strategic About What Questions to Ask

As students become proficient with question words, they'll be ready to use those words to ask questions for specific reasons, such as seeking clarification, requesting an opinion, and digging deeper for greater insight. By understanding the purpose behind every question, students can better clarify their own thinking about which type of question to ask in a given situation.

Introduce the skill. One way to do this teaching is to use a Focused Brainstorm (page 176), as in the following lesson.

→ **Choose a short, engaging text** or video clip for students to read or watch. Then have students form small groups, and give each group a large piece of chart paper.

→ **Have students brainstorm questions** about the text or clip and list them on the chart paper. Remind them to use the question words they learned. When most groups seem to have exhausted their ideas, signal for quiet attention.

→ **Have groups post charts.** Give students a few minutes to walk around and read the charts. If they see interesting questions, they can add them to their group's chart.

→ **Have groups cut up their charts** so that each question is separate. Then invite each group to identify four questions—each serving a different purpose—and bring those back to the whole group. Combine all the questions and lead the class in sorting the questions into categories that reflect the different purposes questions can serve.

→ **Guide the class in labeling each category.** For instance, you might finish with these categories:

- Clarifying questions—to understand what you read, heard, or saw

- Background questions—to understand more about the history behind what you read, heard, or saw

- Questions seeking opinions—to find out what others think about what you read, heard, or saw

- Challenging questions—to find out whether you believe or trust what you read, heard, or saw

Explain that there is no right or wrong set of categories, and that many questions might fit into multiple ones. The value of this activity is getting students to think more deeply and be more strategic with their questions. For a reference students can use in their future academic work, post the categories and some sample questions.

Practice the skill and provide ongoing support. Here are some ideas:

→ **Use a thought-provoking passage.** Have students read the passage (or read it to them) and then analyze it using Numbered Heads Together (page 181) as follows:

- Place the students in small groups and have them count off.

- Instruct each group to brainstorm as many questions as they can that fit a certain question category, such as clarifying questions. Give them three to five minutes for this.

- Call out a number. The student with that number in each group shares out one or two questions from his or her group. Repeat with other types of questions.

→ **Have students analyze or sort textbook or test prep questions** according to what sort of information the question is seeking.

→ **Post and frequently reference anchor charts.** Students may need reminders to use these displays.

> "In your literature circles today, see if your group can discuss at least one of each type of question on our chart."

→ **Pair students up to brainstorm questions.** For example, before having a whole-group conversation about a particular topic, give partners time to think about what questions they have and what their purpose might be in asking those questions.

→ **Have students reflect on the types of questions they've asked.** After any discussion that involves the use of questions, pair them up for a brief reflection on how well they're doing asking questions for specific purposes.

> "Think with your partner for a minute about which types of questions you asked. Which types were easier to think up? Which were harder?"

GIVING HIGH-QUALITY ANSWERS

A clear, concise, and direct answer moves a conversation forward and helps keep it on track, just as an unclear or irrelevant answer can derail one. The ability to answer questions proficiently carries over into all academic subject areas.

Understanding What the Speaker Is Asking

Introduce the skill. Often, students rush to answer a question without first thinking about the question itself. But before students can provide an answer, they must first understand exactly what information the question is asking for. Here's one way to teach students this skill using Interactive Modeling (page 172):

→ **Tell students why the skill matters.**

> "Today we're going to work on answering questions thoughtfully. The first step is to understand exactly what the other person is asking. Notice what I do when Jen asks me a question about my solution to a math problem."

→ **Demonstrate the skill.** Remember to model careful listening skills as in Chapter One (voice off, eyes on the speaker, interested facial expression). Then clearly pause before answering to show that you're clarifying in your head what the student is asking. You may want to do a think-aloud while pointing to your head.

> "During the pause, I wanted to make sure I knew exactly what Jen was asking. I heard her say that she wanted to know what I meant when I said I 'looked for tens.' So I knew my answer had to explain that in more detail."

→ **Invite students to share what they noticed.**

> "What did I do to make sure I answered the question well?"

If needed, prompt students to be sure they noticed how you demonstrated listening (to continue to reinforce those skills), and that you paused and took some time to figure out how to answer the question.

→ **Teach students what to say when they don't understand a question.** In this same lesson or a separate one, brainstorm with students phrases they could use in these situations. You could then use these phrases to create an anchor chart.

Practice the skill and provide ongoing support.

→ **Have students discuss questions in their academic work.** Have partners or small groups work together to reach a common understanding of what written questions, such as questions from a textbook chapter review or test prep exercise, are asking. Prompt students:

"How can you use what we learned about question words to clarify what information these questions are asking you to provide?"

→ **Post anchor charts and remind students to use them.** For instance, before you send students off to discuss a challenging text, you might say:

"Remember to clarify what your partner is asking. You can use the ideas from our anchor chart if you're not sure what to say."

➙ **Focus on pausing.** Some students, especially those who struggle with impulse control, may have difficulty pausing to make sure they understand what the speaker is asking. From time to time, sit with these students to help them with this skill. For example, you might quietly whisper in their ear:

> "Wait, Ariel. Think about what Kimmy is really asking before you answer."

Referring to the Question in the Answer

Introduce the skill. This skill may take longer to develop because students are used to answering questions, especially oral ones, in much less formal ways. But using words from the question in their answer is important because it helps students focus in on exactly what the question is asking and offer a thorough response.

To teach this skill, you can use Interactive Modeling (page 172) as part of an academic lesson on responding to a writing prompt or answering questions in a textbook or on a practice test.

➙ **Set a purpose for the learning.**

> "When we answer questions, we want to make sure our answer is clear to everyone who's reading it or listening in. Watch and see how I do this when Shari asks me a question from our social studies textbook."

➙ **Demonstrate the skill.** Use specific words from the question to begin your answer. For instance, if the question is "What are the names of the five Great Lakes?" answer by saying "The names of the five Great Lakes are Huron, Ontario, Michigan, Erie, and Superior."

➙ **Have students point out what you did.** Make sure students note that you began your answer with the same words that ended the question. You may also want to prompt students to note that you spoke in a complete sentence.

➙ **Ask students to model.** Give them several opportunities to see how it looks to incorporate key parts of the question into the answer—this skill is not as simple as it may seem.

Practice the skill. Make this practice as fun and engaging as you can.

↝ **Use the Swap Meet structure** (page 184) to give students several rounds of practice in quick succession.

- Pose an interesting question to ponder.

> "Based on what we have read about India, what are some specific places there you'd like to visit, and why?"

- Give students a minute to take some quick notes. Then for three to four minutes , have students walk around and share ideas with a few partners while incorporating key words from the question in their answers.

- Point out what you noticed students doing well.

> "I heard many of you using words from my question in your answers. Your answers were easier to follow because you included part of the question in them."

↝ **Practice the skill at morning meetings and other class meetings.** If you have students share personal news and then take questions, remind them to incorporate some of the questioner's words in their responses.

Provide ongoing support. Here are some ideas to try:

↝ **Remind students to use the skill.** For younger students, you may want to do this at the start of every discussion. Older students may need the reminder only when a topic is more difficult or unfamiliar.

> "Who can remind us what we've been learning about answering questions using words from the question?"

→ **Teach students respectful ways to help when a classmate forgets to use the skill.** If students are finding this skill especially challenging, lead them in brainstorming ways they could remind each other.

> I didn't understand your answer. Can you please reword it? Maybe using words from the question would help.

> The question asked for three reasons and you gave two. Would starting your answer with some question words help you give a third reason?

Answering Questions Concisely and Completely

Answers that are both concise and complete bring everyone—the questioner, others listening in, and even the answerer—to higher levels of understanding and drive the conversation forward. To do this requires:

→ **getting to the point quickly**

→ **answering only the question asked**

→ **choosing precise words**

Introduce the skill. To demonstrate what answering a question thoroughly but succinctly looks like, you can use a Fishbowl (page 174) or an Expert Demonstration (page 175). Remember to prepare the student modelers in advance and connect this teaching with what you have already taught about staying on topic in Chapter Two (pages 53–56). Here's how to do this lesson as a Fishbowl demonstration:

→ **Set the stage.**

> "All year, we've been talking about being brief and to the point when speaking. It's just as important to do that when answering questions. Watch how our classmates in the Fishbowl do that as they answer one another's questions about their research projects."

→ **Keep the demonstration engaging.** Invite a student in the Fishbowl to briefly share some research she's been doing on a science project. Have others in the group ask questions. The student then models answering the questions completely but succinctly.

→ **Debrief.** Ask the class what they noticed the student doing.

> "What did you notice about how Kayla answered the questions?"

Be sure students notice that she got to the point quickly, answered only the question asked, and used precise words.

Practice the skill and provide ongoing support. Here are some ideas to try:

→ **Use Inside-Outside Circles** (page 180). Provide a mix of questions, from those that can be answered very briefly ("Where were you born?") to those that require supporting details ("Who is a person you admire, and why?"). Tell students that for this practice, they should consider only what the question asks and try to make their answer precise. As students answer, tell them what they're doing well:

> "I heard many of you stop yourselves after you stated where you were born—even though you could have added details about that place—because that's all the question asked for."

> "I heard many precise words used as you talked about the people you admire. You kept your answer concise by giving just the key reasons."

→ **Pair students up to analyze informational texts.** Have partners take turns asking and answering each other's questions about a social studies, science, or other informational text they've read. Remind them to practice speaking with clarity and brevity.

> "Be sure to respond with just enough detail so that your partner understands your answer, but not so much detail that he or she feels overwhelmed."

→ **Have students watch brief video clips.** Students may be especially interested in analyzing interviews of people on TV and other media. After they watch a clip, have them discuss whether the person answered the questions completely and succinctly.

→ **Have students use quick check-ins.** After a student answers a question, have him or her check in with the student who posed it.

→ **Refer to anchor charts.**

> "Use our anchor chart about main ideas and supporting details when you answer the questions."

See page 109 for an example of a main ideas/supporting details anchor chart.

Giving Meaningful Feedback

Whenever you see students engaged in high-quality questioning or answering, encourage them to keep it up.

PROVIDE FREQUENT REINFORCEMENT

While students are learning how to competently ask and respond to questions, they'll need lots of positive feedback and patient coaching. Some excellent times to provide these are:

⇢ **During academic periods.** If you notice a child asking a classmate thoughtful questions during science, you might say:

> "Zoe, I heard you asking Brendan if he thought your plant would lean the other way if you turned it around in the window. That's exactly the kind of question scientists ask."

⇢ **In social situations.** For example, if you see children asking questions at lunch to find out more about each other, point that out.

> "I heard people asking their lunch partners friendly questions about what they like to do outside of school. Your questions showed that you really cared about getting to know them."

→ **During special events.** When parents and other guests visit or students go on field trips, point out to students when they're demonstrating curiosity.

> "You have a lot of questions for Renee's mom about how to run a pizza parlor. We're learning so much more because of your questions!"

→ **During class gatherings, such as morning meetings.** Encourage students to continue finding out more about what classmates shared.

> "I heard so many questions seeking lots of different information. Some people were trying to clarify what happened in people's stories. Others were trying to figure out how those who shared felt. You're all learning to use questions purposefully."

POINT OUT HOW QUESTIONS LEAD TO DEEPER UNDERSTANDING

As often as possible, tie your feedback into the bigger picture—how thoughtful questions and answers move conversations forward or lead everyone to learn more.

→ **To reinforce the whole class's efforts:**

> "When you asked Tyree relevant questions about his strategy, you helped him better understand how he solved the problem and you also helped us think more deeply about division."

→ **To privately reinforce an individual student's efforts:**

> "When you answered the question about the 'evil character,' you made us consider whether that character was more complex than we first thought. That's what a careful answer does— it opens the door for new insights for everyone."

NAME SPECIFICS

When giving feedback, avoid generalities such as "Great question!" because these don't tell children which specific behavior is effective. Also minimize personal approval such as "I love your answer," which can lead children to focus on gaining your approval, rather than learning the skills. Instead, name what students are specifically doing that's effective or specifically how a behavior will help advance their learning.

Instead of . . .	Try . . .
"What an interesting question!"	"When you asked 'What do scientists suggest we do to keep honeybees from dying off?' you showed that you were really curious about Marco's research." (Give this feedback privately.)
"That is such a great answer!"	"That answer is going to help us explore what the author means. Who else would like to offer an answer to that same question?"
"I like these questions I'm hearing."	"Your questions are focused on the speaker's ideas, and you're using friendly voices."

INCLUDE REFLECTIVE QUESTIONS

By prompting students to do some self-reflecting on their use of questions and answers, they'll deepen their thinking and boost their use of these skills. You can encourage this self-reflection by including a reflective question from time to time when you give feedback.

> "I noticed that people asked 'how' and 'why' questions during science today. How did those types of questions help you understand electric circuits better?"

> "In your literature circles, many of you chose precise words in your answers about when and why the main character said certain things. How did that help you better understand the main character?"

Addressing Common Mistakes

Respond to mistakes students make respectfully, using a neutral tone of voice. Focus on what might help students improve rather than worrying about how they may be hampering the flow of a lesson.

ASKING TOO MANY QUESTIONS

Tips for Addressing Mistakes

✔ **Convey confidence in students' ability** to correct mistakes so that they feel comfortable continuing with their question or answer.

✔ **Be brief and to the point** so that the conversation can keep going.

✔ **Give replacement language** when appropriate (such as a question starter for a student about to go off topic).

For some students, asking questions comes so easily that they inundate speakers with question after question. Speakers may feel overwhelmed, or the questioner might take too much time. Remember not to shut such students down completely: Their curiosity is a positive attribute to be fostered. Instead, help them focus and prioritize.

⇢ **Encourage them to pick their top two questions.**

> "Liam, it sounds as if you're really interested in what Sophia has to say. For now, think about your two most important questions and ask just those."

⇢ **Provide ideas for when they can continue the conversation.**

> "Ava, you seem so interested in Marc's math project. I'll give you five minutes at the end of math for you to ask him more questions. If that's not enough, you can keep talking at lunch, if Marc is OK with that."

OFF-THE-MARK ANSWERS

At times, speakers may seem to mishear or ignore what they were asked. As a result, they may not answer the question that was actually asked or may answer in a vague way. For instance, a student discussing what she plans to write during writers' workshop might respond to the question "Where will the story take place?" by saying, "It's going to be a really spooky story with lots of characters."

When students are having trouble zeroing in on the question asked, try these strategies:

→ **Stop the speaker gently.** Then, coach her on what to do differently.

> "Stop and think about what words Jaden used and exactly what information he was asking for. Ask a clarifying question if you need to."

→ **Have the questioner ask again.** Then focus the speaker's attention on key words in the question.

> "It sounds as if Jaden really is interested in the setting—where it will take place. So what kind of place might be spooky?"

Essential Skills at a Glance

ASKING AND ANSWERING QUESTIONS	
Core Question Skills (pages 75–79)	→ Know the difference between a question and a statement. → Ask questions respectfully.

Asking Purposeful Questions (pages 79–84)	→ Ask questions for specific purposes, such as for clarification or further explanation.
	 → Recognize and use question words to ask questions purposefully:
	   • Who
	   • What
	   • Where
	   • When
	   • Why.
	   • How

Giving High-Quality Answers (pages 85–91)	→ Understand what the speaker is asking. → Refer to the question in the answer. → Answer the question concisely and completely.

Sample Letter to Parents

Dear Parents,

We're working on making our academic conversations rich and productive. Most recently, we've been working on asking relevant questions and answering questions clearly. Questions lie at the heart of learning, so these are crucial skills for students to develop. Getting better at asking and answering questions will help your child in all subjects—science, math, reading, writing, and social studies. I'd like to share a few simple ideas for practicing these skills at home:

- Try to be open to questions. I know how hard this can be, especially because children don't always ask questions at convenient times. But the more we can encourage children to be curious, the better learners they'll be. If you don't have time to answer a question, have your child write it down so you can answer it later (this can help with writing, too!).

- Play games that encourage questions. One we've been enjoying at school is 20 Questions. You can play it with any topic. For instance, think of a famous person and have your child ask you up to 20 yes-or-no questions to try to figure out who it is.

- Point out when your child asks an interesting or thought-provoking question. For instance, at school, I might privately say to a child, "When you asked how trees can grow from seedless oranges, you showed you were thinking scientifically, and you gave all of us a new direction for our research!"

And, as always, if you have any questions, please contact me. Thank you for supporting your child's learning!

Crafting an Argument

Organized, Well-Supported, Convincing

Students need to know how to state facts and express their opinions effectively so that they can positively contribute to classroom conversations and so that their classmates seriously consider their ideas. To present information and ideas well—and to craft them into an effective argument—students have to use a number of skills and do so in concert, as they do in this scene from a first grade classroom.

The students have just read a classic fairy tale, Hansel and Gretel. Their discussion reveals that many children think the stepmother and the witch acted cruelly. Wanting to push their thinking a little further, the teacher asks, "What about the father?" She gives them time to think and then has them share with a partner while she circulates to listen in and coach as needed.

One of the students she observes, Shauna, is asserting a strong point of view: "I believe the father did a bad thing. He should have told the stepmother 'no.' It doesn't matter how much the stepmother pestered him. He's supposed to take care of his kids. He is a grown-up. He didn't have to do what she said. My father would never do that to me!" Her partner Arianne nods her head, clearly struck by Shauna's argument.

Common Core Connections · · · · · **103**

How to Teach the Skills:

  Organizing Thoughts · · · · · · · · **107**
  *Distinguishing Facts From
    Opinions* · · · · · · · · · · · · · · · **113**
  Presenting Evidence · · · · · · · · **119**
  Persuading Others · · · · · · · · · · **122**

Giving Meaningful Feedback · · · · **125**

Addressing Common Mistakes · · **128**

_____

Essential Skills at a Glance · · · · · · · **132**

Sample Letter to Parents · · · · · · · **133**

Shauna's skills in presenting her argument—identifying what she was saying as her opinions ("I believe") and then backing up her opinions with references to the text and her own experiences—are no doubt impressive for a first grader. But it's important to remember that all children can learn how to present information and opinions effectively.

Shauna's teacher deliberately taught her class these skills. With careful teaching, even students as young as Shauna and her classmates can become capable speakers.

In this chapter, you'll learn about the skills students need to present information and assert their ideas respectfully—organizing their thoughts, distinguishing fact from opinion, supporting their opinions, and then putting all of these together to form persuasive arguments. You'll also learn concrete ideas for how to teach these skills, ways for students to practice them, and tips for supporting students on their road to proficiency.

Why These Skills Matter

Presenting information and ideas effectively is critical to students' success in academic conversations and beyond because these skills:

→ **Boost students' critical thinking abilities.** Teaching students to organize what they say, recognize if they're asserting a fact or an opinion, and support what they say with reasons and evidence helps students clarify their thinking, a key to academic success.

→ **Lead to higher-level conversations.** When students can provide new information and insights, be assertive yet respectful, and offer persuasive arguments when appropriate, academic conversations are enriched and everyone benefits.

→ **Support success in all subject areas.** The skills in this chapter can help students succeed in language arts, science, social studies, and math. For instance, students who can state a clear position and build a logical case for it in conversation are much more likely to be able to write an effective argument.

→ **Prepare students for more formal speaking situations.** Although this chapter primarily addresses academic conversation skills, learning these will also enable students to create more effective presentations and speeches—and deliver them more skillfully.

→ **Help deepen and strengthen students' relationships.** Children who can articulate their thinking clearly and, when appropriate, persuasively, will be better equipped to discuss issues that arise in social settings. Doing so capably will also make classroom relationships stronger—and the stronger those relationships, the richer children's learning.

Common Core Connections

Kindergarten

SL.K.1: Participate in collaborative conversations with diverse partners about kindergarten topics and texts.

SL.K.1a: Follow agreed-upon rules for discussions (e.g., listening to others and taking turns speaking).

SL.K.4: Describe familiar people, places, things, and events and, with prompting and support, provide additional detail.

SL.K.6: Speak audibly and express thoughts, feelings, and ideas clearly.

1st Grade

SL.1.1: Participate in collaborative conversations with diverse partners about grade 1 topics and texts.

SL.1.1a: Follow agreed-upon rules for discussions (e.g., listening to others with care, speaking one at a time).

SL.1.1b: Build on others' talk in conversations by responding to the comments of others through multiple exchanges.

SL.1.4: Describe people, places, things, and events with relevant details, expressing ideas and feelings clearly.

SL.1.6: Produce complete sentences when appropriate to task and situation.

2nd Grade

SL.2.1: Participate in collaborative conversations with diverse partners about grade 2 topics and texts.

SL.2.1a: Follow agreed-upon rules for discussions (e.g., gaining the floor in respectful ways, listening with care, speaking one at a time).

SL.2.1b: Build on others' talk in conversations by linking their comments to the remarks of others.

SL.2.2: Recount or describe key ideas or details from a text read aloud or information presented orally or through other media.

SL.2.4: Tell a story or recount an experience with appropriate facts and relevant, descriptive details, speaking audibly in coherent sentences.

SL.2.6: Produce complete sentences when appropriate to task and situation.

Speaking and Listening Standards Supported in Chapter Four

3rd Grade

SL.3.1: Engage effectively in a range of collaborative discussions (one-on-one, in groups, and teacher-led) with diverse partners on grade 3 topics and texts.

SL.3.1a: Come to discussions prepared.

SL.3.1b: Follow agreed-upon rules for discussions (e.g., gaining the floor in respectful ways, listening to others with care, speaking one at a time).

SL.3.2: Determine the main ideas and supporting details of a text read aloud or information presented in diverse media and formats.

SL.3.4: Report on a topic or text, tell a story, or recount an experience with appropriate facts and relevant, descriptive details, speaking clearly at an understandable pace.

SL.3.6: Speak in complete sentences when appropriate to task and situation in order to provide requested detail or clarification.

4th Grade

SL.4.1: Engage effectively in a range of collaborative discussions (one-on-one, in groups, and teacher-led) with diverse partners on grade 4 topics and texts.

SL.4.1a: Come to discussions prepared.

SL.4.1b: Follow agreed-upon rules for discussions and carry out assigned roles.

SL.4.2. Paraphrase portions of a text read aloud or information presented in diverse media and formats.

SL.4.4: Report on a topic or text, tell a story, or recount an experience in an organized manner, using appropriate facts and relevant, descriptive details to support main ideas or themes; speak clearly at an understandable pace.

SL.4.6: Differentiate between contexts that call for formal English and situations where informal discourse is appropriate; use formal English when appropriate to task and situation.

5th Grade

SL.5.1: Engage effectively in a range of collaborative discussions (one-on-one, in groups, and teacher-led) with diverse partners on grade 5 topics and texts.

SL.5.1a: Come to discussions prepared.

SL.5.1b: Follow agreed-upon rules for discussions and carry out assigned roles.

SL.5.1d: Review the key ideas expressed and draw conclusions in light of information and knowledge gained from the discussions.

SL.5.2: Summarize a written text read aloud or information presented in diverse media and formats.

SL.5.4: Report on a topic or text or present an opinion, sequencing ideas logically and using appropriate facts and relevant, descriptive details to support main ideas or themes; speak clearly at an understandable pace.

SL.5.6: Adapt speech to a variety of contexts and tasks, using formal English when appropriate to task and situation.

6th Grade

SL.6.1: Engage effectively in a range of collaborative discussions (one-on-one, in groups, and teacher-led) with diverse partners on grade 6 topics, texts, and issues.

SL.6.1a: Come to discussions prepared.

SL.6.1b: Follow rules for collegial discussions.

SL.6.1d: Review the key ideas expressed and demonstrate understanding of multiple perspectives through reflection and paraphrasing.

SL.6.2: Interpret information presented in diverse media and formats and explain how it contributes to a topic, text, or issue under study.

SL.6.4: Present claims and findings, sequencing ideas logically and using pertinent descriptions, facts, and details to accentuate main ideas or themes; use appropriate eye contact, adequate volume, and clear pronunciation.

SL.6.6: Adapt speech to a variety of contexts and tasks, demonstrating command of formal English when indicated or appropriate.

How to Teach the Skills

Here are some guidelines to keep in mind as you teach students how to state information convincingly and respectfully:

> **Four skills crucial to crafting an argument**
>
> ✔ **Speaking in an organized way**
>
> ✔ **Distinguishing facts from opinions**
>
> ✔ **Presenting evidence**
>
> ✔ **Persuading others**

→ **Point out when you use the skills.** Students learn speaking and listening skills from their parents, teachers, and other adults in their lives. From time to time while you teach, briefly but explicitly tell students when you're organizing your thoughts, telling fact from opinion, or using reasons and evidence.

→ **Consider children's developmental stages.** This chapter covers a wide variety of skills, some of which are quite advanced. Have high but realistic expectations for your students. For instance, first graders can organize their thoughts with a main idea and a few supporting details, but they'll need much more practice and support in differentiating between a fact and an opinion than a fifth grader would.

→ **Keep in mind children's cultural backgrounds.** If you're teaching skills that might conflict with a child's home culture, remember to explain that they can support success in school, college, and the workplace, and be patient as students develop them.

→ **Teach skills progressively.** Begin with the ones that students need to use during the first weeks of school—typically, recounting events or experiences in an organized and sequential way. Once students gain competency with those, start adding skills based on what your students need next, depending on your grade level and curriculum.

→ **Connect to academics frequently.** Whenever possible, combine instruction in these speaking skills with your academic lessons, such as when you're teaching younger students how to write opinion pieces or older students how to write effective arguments.

For a suggested timeline of when to teach academic conversation skills throughout the school year, see page 191.

SPEAKING IN AN ORGANIZED WAY

Students often need to speak about topics at some length. For example, they may be called on to recount personal or academic experiences or describe people, places, things, or events. To be comprehensible, students need to organize what they want to say as if they were making mini-presentations. Here are the specific skills they need to learn:

→ **using main ideas and supporting details**

→ **sequencing ideas logically** (first this happened, then this, and so on)

Using Main Ideas and Supporting Details

Introduce the skill. Because clearly stating a main idea and including relevant details does not come naturally to most children, they need to be taught this skill. One way to do this is to use Interactive Modeling (page 172).

→ **State the learning goal** to be sure students understand the point of what you're about to demonstrate.

> "Today, as part of science, you'll present information about your solar system topic to a small group. It's important to do this in an organized way so that listeners can understand you. I'm going to show you one way to organize information. Watch and see what I do."

→ **Demonstrate with a simple example.**

> "I'd like to share some interesting facts about Mercury. It's the closest planet to the sun, but it's still 36 million miles away! It's very hot on the side that faces the sun and really cold on the other side. Its year is only 88 days compared to 365 on Earth. Mercury is less than half the size of Earth."

→ **Guide students to point out key aspects** of what you demonstrated. Begin with an open-ended question.

> "What did you notice about how I organized my information?"

If students do not point out your use of a main idea and supporting details, prompt them:

- "What did I say first? How did that sentence help you as listeners?" (main idea)

- "What sorts of facts did I share about Mercury?" "About how many?" "Why is it important to choose only a few key details?" (supporting details)

Use what students noticed in this discussion to make an anchor chart for their reference in future discussions. (See the opposite page for a sample chart.)

→ **Invite a student to demonstrate** using a main idea and supporting details. After he or she models the skills, ask students what they noticed, prompting them as needed. Then place students in small groups and let each share in the same way about their solar system topic.

Practice the skill. Because using a main idea and supporting details is so foundational for students' academic work, give them many opportunities to present information with this same "main idea first—supporting details later" format. For instance, students could:

→ **Present a brief book summary.** Invite a few students at a time to give "book talks"—brief summaries of a book they read recently and why they liked it—to give other students ideas for what they might want to read next.

→ **Preview their writing during writers' workshop.** Have students conduct a brief conversation with a classmate in which they lay out the main topic and supporting details about a piece of writing they're working on.

→ **Share personal news during a morning meeting.**

For instance, invite students to share about a special family tradition, reminding them about using main ideas and supporting details.

One of our family's traditions is Friday movie night. Almost every Friday night we get together and watch a DVD. My grandparents let us have a snack while we watch. We take turns choosing the movie.

After students share, point out what the sharers did well:

"You told us your main idea right away. That helped us understand exactly what you were going to talk about. Then you told us a few key details, which gave us a clear picture of your family tradition."

Provide ongoing support.

Because these skills can be challenging to learn, support students as they practice so that they'll encounter little successes along the way to mastery. Here are some tips:

→ **Post an anchor chart.**

Keep this chart handy for times when students will be speaking at greater length and add to it as their skills progress.

Using Main Ideas and Supporting Details

* Present your main idea first.

* Give important details next (at least two, no more than four).

* Use who, what, when, where, how, and why details.

→ **Have students use notes.** For certain assignments or for additional support for some students, have them bring notes of their main idea and key details to the conversation. During a weather unit, for instance, students might bring notes on their reading about different types of severe weather to help them briefly present to a small group as shown in the example below:

Main Idea: Tornadoes are powerful storms.

Details: * powerful rotating cylinder of air

* result from unstable mixture of warm, moist air from the Gulf of Mexico and cool, dry air from Canada

* can occur anywhere in the U.S., but more common in Midwest and South

* cause much damage to property and can be deadly

→ **Provide concrete reminders.** Younger students and even some older ones may benefit from tangible ways of remembering how to organize their thoughts. For instance, I give kindergartners four linking math cubes before they speak. The first, a different color from the other three, represents the main idea. The next three, all the same color, represent the details. As children speak, they put the cubes in front of them to help them remember how to use a main idea and supporting details (and to remind themselves how much to say).

→ **Have students practice ahead of time.** With students who find public speaking situations especially daunting or for those just learning English, have them practice with you ahead of time. Or have them practice with a classmate, student in an upper grade, or family member at home.

Sequencing Ideas Logically

Introduce the skill. Sometimes students need to present information in a logical, sequential order so their listeners can understand them, such as when describing a historical event or explaining how they solved a math problem. To teach them this skill, try using Interactive Modeling (page 172) as in the following example.

⇢ **Say what you'll model and why.**

> "Sometimes when we're sharing, we need to present information in order. An example would be the sequence of events when a seed grows into a plant. Notice how I do that as I describe the life cycle of a cactus."

⇢ **Model the behavior.**

> "In *Cactus Hotel* by Brenda Z. Guiberson, I learned that the life cycle of a saguaro cactus begins when a seed falls from a cactus flower. The seed grows into a small plant. Next, after a long time, branches grow. Then animals nest in the cactus, which is why it's called a 'cactus hotel.' Finally, after about 150 years, the cactus dies."

⇢ **Ask students what they noticed.**

> "What did you notice about how I described the life cycle?"

Be sure students notice that you began with what happened first and then moved in order to the next important event. Also call their attention to the words you used to show sequence (*begins, next, then, finally*). You may want to make an anchor chart of these words for future use.

⇢ **Give students a chance to practice.** Have students tell partners about the life cycle of a plant or animal. As they share, point out what they're doing well in terms of sequencing.

> "We all now have a clear mental picture of how a tomato plant grows because you went in order, starting with the seed and concluding with how the tomatoes form."

Practice the skill. To help children move toward proficiency with these skills, give them plenty of opportunities for meaningful practice. Try to vary the practice context as well, so that they can develop these skills across the curriculum. In addition to using the practice structures outlined on pages 177–186, try these two suggestions:

→ **Presenting solutions to math problems.** Invite students to share their thinking or approach to a given math problem, reminding them to think in terms of the order of their steps.

> "Remember, your strategy will make more sense to listeners if you go in order."

→ **Giving directions for a procedure.** Assign students to write "how to" books or directions for an everyday task such as building a structure out of clay. As a mini-lesson leading up to this writing, have students orally tell the key steps to a partner, who carries out each step as it's named. Both students can see from the results just how clear and specific the directions were.

Provide ongoing support. Placing events or steps in the correct sequence isn't as straightforward as it seems, even for adults. To help ensure students' success, pay attention to the whole group's progress and that of individual students, providing support as needed.

→ **Use anchor charts.** Remind students to use these charts as they work. For example, before students begin a writing assignment that requires sequential order, refer them to a chart like the one shown here.

How to Put Events in Order

* Start with main idea.

* Tell what happened first, second, third, and so on.

* Conclude with what took place last.

* Choose only the most important steps to include.

→ **Help students use notes and graphic organizers.** When students need to share about more complex processes or are just gaining experience speaking in public, encourage them to prepare notes or a graphic organizer (like the one at right) to help them present information in a sequential way. Remind them that even the best public speakers use notes when giving a speech!

Sentence Starters for Putting Events in Order

"The first thing that happened was _____."

"Next, _____."

"Then, _____."

"Finally, _____."

→ **Have students work with partners.** Prior to presenting the sequence of events or steps in a process, students often benefit from a quick check-in with a partner to make sure they have understood the correct order. These brief check-ins can help boost students' confidence before they speak to the whole group.

DISTINGUISHING FACTS FROM OPINIONS

For success in school, students need to know the difference between facts and opinions—and how to make that distinction clear as they speak. Speakers build trust in their listeners when they indicate whether they're speaking factually or just offering their opinion. These are the key skills for students to learn:

→ **knowing what's a fact and what's an opinion**—and how to tell the difference between them

→ **presenting facts** in a way that tells listeners the information can be verified

→ **presenting opinions** in a way that tells listeners these are the speaker's personal beliefs

Building a conversation and keeping the learning going requires that every student involved in a classroom discussion knows how to use all these skills simultaneously.

For Younger Students

Introduce the skill. Try using two slightly modified Interactive Modeling lessons (page 172) on separate days. On the first day, introduce skills related to presenting factual information. On the second, introduce skills related to expressing opinions.

↪ **To introduce speaking factually, state what you'll model and why.**

"When we're speaking, it's important to let listeners know when we're talking about facts—real things that happened and that we can prove. Watch how I do that using one of our sentence starters."

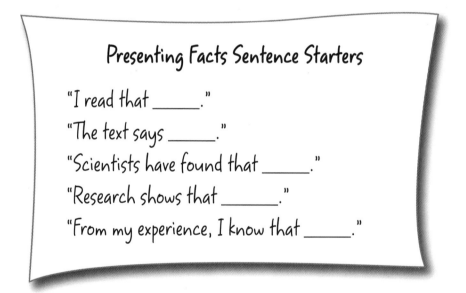

Presenting Facts Sentence Starters

"I read that _____."

"The text says _____."

"Scientists have found that _____."

"Research shows that _____."

"From my experience, I know that _____."

↪ **To introduce expressing opinions,** also state what you'll model and why.

"Yesterday, we talked about sharing facts. But sometimes we'll also want to share our opinions, which are our personal beliefs—for example, why we think a character made a certain decision. I'm going to use one of our sentence starters to give an opinion."

Expressing Opinions Sentence Starters

"I think _____." "I believe _____." "In my opinion, _____."

→ **For each lesson, make sure students notice key aspects of the statement.**

> "How did I let my listeners know that I was sharing a fact, not just an idea I had?"

> "How did I let my listeners know that I was sharing my opinion, not something that was factually true?"

→ **Before students practice these skills, do a quick review with them,** asking them first for statements that are facts and then for statements of opinion about a given topic. For example:

Dog Facts	Dog Opinions
• Dogs are mammals.	• Dogs are good companions.
• Dogs have fur.	• Dogs are cuddly.
• Dogs have four legs and a tail.	• Dogs are dangerous.
• Some dogs help people.	• Dogs are better pets than cats.

→ **Have students practice with partners.** Name a new topic and have students practice sharing fact and opinion statements together. Direct them to use the sentence starters you modeled and the chart the class created together for support.

For Older Students

Introduce fact and opinion statements in combination by using a Fishbowl lesson (page 174):

→ **Prepare students who'll be in the Fishbowl.** Do a quick practice in advance, making sure the demonstrators clearly know the difference between factual statements and opinions, and how to use appropriate sentence starters to state one or the other. Use a topic your students have been studying recently. One fourth grade teacher had her Fishbowl students discuss measurement in connection with math.

→ **Have the class take notes as they watch.** Prompt them to notice how the speakers signaled when they were giving factual statements and when they were giving opinions. After the demonstration, you may want to have students review their notes with a partner.

→ **List statements of fact and opinion.** Have individuals share with the whole class one factual statement and one opinion they heard.

> Sara said that she measured her desk with the meter stick and that it was 61 centimeters wide and 45 centimeters long. Those are facts because we can prove them.

> When John said that his desk last year was better than his desk this year, he was giving an opinion because it was his personal belief, rather than a fact that we could prove.

Practice the skill. Both younger and older students will benefit from regular practice, which can easily be built in to class discussions and academic lessons. For example:

→ **Practice at morning meetings.** As a few students share personal news each morning, encourage them from time to time to use sentence starters to indicate which of their statements are factual and which are opinions. For instance, a student might share a story like this:

> Last night, I had to go to the emergency room because I fell off my bike. I thought it was a scary place because it was so noisy. I had to have an X-ray and then the doctor put my arm in a cast.

After each student shares, have listeners identify statements that were facts and those that were opinions.

→ **Analyze passages from a newspaper or magazine.** Have students work with partners to choose some factual statements and some opinions from an assigned text to share with the class.

→ **Use Circle Maps.** One fun way for students to get experience with the difference between factual statements and opinions is by using Circle Maps (page 177):

1. **Place students in small groups.** Give each group a large chart-sized piece of paper and markers.

2. **Have them draw a large circle on the paper.** In the middle of the circle, they write their group's assigned topic. (You can either give each group a different topic or have all groups work on the same topic.)

3. **Invite students to brainstorm about the topic,** recording everything they've read or think they know about it inside the big circle. After five minutes or so, signal for quiet attention.

4. Direct students to:

- circle any statement that's a fact, and write a source that could be used to verify it

- place a rectangle around any statement that's an opinion

- draw a triangle next to any statement they're uncertain about

5. Have groups switch charts. The new group members put checks next to any designation with which they agree and question marks next to any they question.

Provide ongoing support. As students begin learning to distinguish fact from opinion and to present facts and opinions in their classroom conversations, reinforce what they're doing well and address what they need more help with. Support both the whole group and individual students as needed. Here are some tips:

→ **Frequently refer to anchor charts** (pages 114–115).

"In your literature circles today, be sure to clarify whether you're sharing something that really happened in the book or sharing your opinion. Remember to use our anchor charts if you need them."

→ **Use prompting questions.** If students are unclear about whether a statement is a fact or opinion, ask them to clarify their thinking for themselves.

"Is that something you know to be true, or is it your personal belief?"

PRESENTING EVIDENCE

After gaining competence in presenting facts and opinions, students in first grade and up can learn to strengthen their statements, speeches, and presentations by giving evidence to support their ideas. Understanding how to present evidence effectively when speaking will also boost students' proficiency with similar skills in writing.

Introduce the skill. Together as a class, generate criteria for convincing evidence. One way to do this is to use children's books, essays, or speeches from history and guide the class in analyzing what make evidence effective. Here's an example of this instruction from a second grade teacher:

→ **Use an engaging, accessible text.** This teacher chose Mo Willems's book *Don't Let the Pigeon Stay Up Late*. After reading the book to students, she posted sentence strips on which she had written all the reasons the pigeon gave to support his argument that he should be allowed to stay up late.

→ **Categorize the reasons.** The teacher led her students in sorting the pigeon's reasons into categories as follows:

Not Effective	Somewhat Effective	Most Effective
• His stuffed bunny also wants to stay up late. • He is in the mood for a hot dog party. • He wants to count the stars. • It's the middle of the day in China.	• There is an educational program about birds on TV. • He wants to spend time talking with you. • He'll go to bed early tomorrow.	• Studies show that pigeons hardly need any sleep.

→ **Guide students in drawing conclusions.** The teacher then encouraged her students to draw conclusions from their sorting about why certain reasons or evidence are most effective. They created this list for future reference:

Because this learning process is quite complex, especially for young children, you may want to repeat this lesson several times and add to the criteria list.

Practice the skill. Becoming proficient at presenting evidence effectively requires students to practice in multiple, meaningful ways. Make this practice as authentic as possible—for example, connect it to science and social studies ex-plorations, research projects, and literature discussions. Here are some ideas to try:

→ **Use practice structures** such as Inside-Outside Circles (page 180). Students work with partners to explore a common research topic or question, such as "Are some ocean creatures mammals?" As partners share ideas, refer them to the anchor chart you created (see above) and encourage them to be spe-cific when presenting evidence to support their answer to the question.

→ **Provide a problem or challenge** and let students investigate it. For instance, pose a real-life school challenge:

"Our class can get a pet, but first we need to investigate which type to get. This pet must be small, easy to take care of, not too expensive, and safe for school. What would be a good choice for a pet, and why? Be ready to share reasons and evidence for your recommendation."

Place students in small groups and have them work together to investigate. Then have a class discussion in which groups present their findings and rec-ommendations. As students support their statements with evidence, point out how doing so helps everyone make a good decision:

> "It was helpful that many groups investigated how expensive pet food can be. When Rodrigo's group said that a turtle can be fed inexpensively, many people started to lean toward a turtle as our class pet."

→ **Share at morning meeting.** For instance, invite a few students each day to share about which body part from another animal they would like to have for themselves and why it would be helpful. Listeners could give feedback to each student about which statements they found most convincing.

→ **Hold book talks.** Have students try to convince classmates to read a book they love by presenting a summary of the book and why it's a "must read." Then point out the ways students made effective cases for their books.

> "I heard lots of readers using what they knew people liked as reasons for trying their 'must read' books. Connecting to what listeners care about is one way to make a convincing argument."

Provide ongoing support. It's not unusual for students to struggle with this learning process, perhaps forgetting to present all their evidence or still getting facts and opinions mixed up. To support students' growth with these skills:

→ **Create an anchor chart** and reference it as needed. For instance:

> "Today, we're going to discuss whether wolves should be a protected species. Be ready to present your evidence. Refer to our chart, if you need to."

Backing Up Our Ideas

* Use what we learned at school.
* Tell which book (and page, if you can) you learned a fact from.
* Share research (yours or someone else's).

→ **Remind students to bring supporting materials** to conversations as appropriate. Remembering which source they learned a particular fact from can be hard for some students, so let them bring research notes, books they found helpful, or pages printed from reliable websites to discussions in which presenting evidence is likely to be necessary.

PERSUADING OTHERS

As was true in the Hansel and Gretel scene that opened this chapter, even young students can learn to present a persuasive argument. Students of any age can also learn how to analyze an argument in terms of its strong and weak points. Of course, the older your students are, the more in-depth you can go with these skills.

Introduce the skill. Begin this teaching by briefly giving students a "big picture" view of what makes a persuasive argument. Touch on how speakers use their voice and body language to persuade, how they organize their thoughts, and how they offer reasons and evidence for their opinions. To teach students about these aspects of making persuasive arguments, use a Fishbowl (page 174) or Expert Demonstration (page 175).

Here's how one fourth grade teacher uses an Expert Demonstration to teach part of a science unit:

→ **Show a relevant video clip.** The year before, this teacher had videotaped her students once they became skilled with making persuasive arguments. She filmed them debating the issue of how much recycling helps the environment. She chose a particularly instructive segment of the video to show to her current students, who are now also studying recycling.

→ **State the purpose for this learning.** This teacher said:

> "Today, we're going to learn what makes speakers more persuasive. I'm going to show a clip of some students from last year. See which speakers you think are persuasive, and why. Pay attention to their voices, bodies, and words."

→ **Ask what the class noticed.** Among other things, this teacher's students observed the following:

- Speakers who stated their position right away really engaged their attention.

- They found speakers who gave supporting facts more convincing.

- It helped when speakers noted where they got their information.

- Most speakers talked forcefully but not rudely. Because they really seemed to believe what they said, they were very compelling.

→ **Create an anchor chart.** The teacher used what her students noticed as a starting point for making an anchor chart (see below) and then added to it as they learned new skills and nuances.

Persuasive Speakers Use Their . . .

Voices	Bodies	Words
• Are firm but not rude. • Sound like they think they're right, but also listen to others.	• Use hands to make points, but not in a disrespectful way. • Get excited sometimes, but stay in control.	• Give opinions first. • Provide reasons and evidence. • Note source of information.

Practice the skill. Because making a persuasive argument doesn't come naturally to many students, set up comfortable and engaging practices.

→ **Have partners use Pros and Cons** (page 183) to debate.

- Read aloud a statement of opinion based on something your class has been studying. For instance, "The invention of cars has been positive for humans."

- Give everyone a minute or two to think. Then have each student use the guidelines you established to make a brief, persuasive case. (Refer students to an anchor chart like the one above.)

- Debrief with the whole class to discuss ways their partners were particularly persuasive. Add to your anchor chart as appropriate.

→ **Use small group structures** such as Maître d' (page 180) or Numbered Heads Together (page 181). For instance, in Numbered Heads Together students form groups and each group chooses one thing they would like to change to make school a better learning environment. Each group then brainstorms how to persuade the other groups to support their idea. Call on one representative from each group to make their group's case.

Encourage students to use the skills they've been working on:

> "Who can remind us of some things your group needs to do so you can make a persuasive case?"

→ **Show clips from news reports and talk shows** as examples of what persuasion looks and sounds like in real life, perhaps as part of a media literacy unit. After watching the clips, discuss what the speakers said and did that was most and least effective.

Provide ongoing support. The skills required for making an effective argument take time to master, yet they're essential for students' success in every academic area. Here are some ways to boost students' growth with these skills:

→ **Use anchor charts.** Continue adding to the anchor chart as you or students notice other things effective speakers do. Refer to the chart each time students are about to engage in situations calling for the use of persuasion.

→ **Have students practice with partners.** Often, students can present a more persuasive case if they have a chance to reflect, share ideas, and practice with a classmate first. Before lengthier or more complex discussions, pause and give students a chance to do this kind of conferring.

→ **Remind students to prepare ahead of time.** Students will be more successful in making a persuasive argument during classroom discussions if you tell them the topic and give them a chance to think about it in advance (whenever possible).

Giving Meaningful Feedback

For students to become proficient with these skills, they need to "see" their progress. As often as you can, point out what they're doing well.

BE CLEAR

Be as specific as possible when you give feedback, detailing exactly how children are organizing their speech, presenting facts and opinions appropriately, and supporting opinions with evidence. Your clarity of feedback will also serve as a model for the skills you're teaching. Here are some tips:

→ **Describe what students have done well.** To make your description even more meaningful, tie it in to anchor charts or discussion criteria whenever possible. For instance, you might point to an anchor chart that lists key ways to be persuasive and say:

> "You provided three statements from the text to support your argument that European colonization hurt indigenous populations in North America. You're using evidence effectively and that helps you make a convincing argument!"

→ **Reinforce the whole group's efforts.** Hearing the ways their contributions lead to learning for the whole class helps students as a learning community.

> "In our math discussions, we learned four ways to figure out this shape's area. I heard many speakers explain how they solved the problem, step-by-step. We now have a clear picture of each strategy, and that will enable us to make a better choice about which one to use next time."

When giving feedback to individual students, remember to do so in private.

LOOK FOR POSITIVES IN EACH STUDENT

Some students may catch on to these skills more readily than others. Point out those students' successes, but also be sure to look for and name positives in students who are finding these skills more challenging.

→ **Reaffirm your belief in each student's abilities**. Send a message with your feedback that all children can learn these skills. Many children fall into a trap of thinking that they're just not good at expressing their ideas or speaking in public. Use language that fosters an understanding that hard work, not genetics or luck, leads to success.

> "Today when you shared, you presented your main idea first and three relevant details. I can tell that you've been working hard on organizing your thoughts and presenting them clearly."

→ **Celebrate partial successes.** Help children recognize the importance of progress toward a larger goal. Name what they did well and point out where their partial successes can lead.

> "You stated your conclusion very clearly. Everyone knew that, in your opinion, new technologies are not always helpful. That's a crucial step in being persuasive—if you know what your main point is, then you can communicate it effectively."

HELP STUDENTS SELF-EVALUATE

Help students reflect on their progress, as a class or individually, in learning the skills of presenting information and ideas.

→ **Encourage them to focus on what they're doing well.** Without your guidance, students may criticize themselves or their classmates. Instead, direct their attention to the skills they're using effectively and how their work has helped the class.

> "Let's look at our anchor chart and check how well we've been doing with persuasive speaking. Which criteria do you think we've been meeting regularly?"

→ **Use open-ended questions to guide reflection.** Ask questions that have no "right" answer and that will prompt students to think and talk about their successes.

> "What did we do well today in terms of supporting our opinions with strong reasons and evidence? How did that help our understanding of the book?"

> "How did we help our listeners fully understand the stories we're reading?"

> "What's one thing speakers did in our conversations today that helped you understand their opinions?"

Addressing Common Mistakes

Remember to keep your expectations realistic and developmentally appropriate. Try to step in and address mistakes at just the right time. You don't want to intervene too soon nor let students flounder too long.

TOO MUCH DETAIL

Children often struggle in deciding which details are relevant. Often, they go for a "more is better" approach. Cutting them off can feel uncomfortable, but if you let students continue for too long, they won't grow as speakers—and listeners will tune them out. To help students who talk too long:

→ **Respectfully stop them.**

> "Alex, you gave us three details. Stop there so you can take questions and comments."

→ **Use a visual cue.** To help a student who struggles with knowing when to stop, use an anchor chart as a visual cue, or prearrange with the student a specific visual cue. For example, you might put up a finger for each point the student makes and then nod when he's reached the maximum.

Tips for Addressing Mistakes

✔ **Use a supportive tone** that lets the student know you're there not to critique but to help.

✔ **Give feedback succinctly.** Tell students what to do instead of what not to do.

✔ **Let students know why the skill matters** (when possible).

TOO ARGUMENTATIVE

Some students may state their points in ways that feel too dismissive or confrontational. For instance, a student might say in a strident tone, "I don't see how anyone could believe that Abraham Lincoln was not a great president!"

→ **Presume positive intentions.** You may want to protect other students' feelings, but try to avoid this reaction. Instead, view the argumentative student's passion as a sign of engagement and help him redirect that passion more productively.

→ **Help the student try again.** As specifically as possible, give the student a strategy for getting back on track. For instance, in the example above, you might say:

> "Brendan, begin again with a more respectful tone, and try using 'In my opinion' or another one of our sentence starters."

INSUFFICIENT FACTS

Children often form opinions with no or only partial reference to facts. They may do so because they have a fuzzy memory of the facts or because they're still trying to understand how to support opinions with reasons and evidence. To give them a chance to back up what they have to say:

→ **Ask a respectful, open-ended question.** Sometimes children can come up with a reason or fact in response to a gentle query.

> "What's already happened in the book that makes you think the engine can't help the broken train make it over the mountain?"

→ **Provide concrete ideas of where to find information.** Instead of ignoring or dismissing an unsupported opinion, suggest a resource the student can use for backup. For example:

> "Mariel, remember to use text references to support your prediction of what will happen next. Take a minute and look through the chapter to see if you can find any evidence that supports your prediction."

UNORGANIZED OR ILLOGICAL PRESENTATION

At times, children may present events out of sequence, omit key details, presume listeners already know certain facts, or make an incoherent argument. To help these students:

→ **Ask leading questions.** If you think you have a sense of where the student is headed, help him get there.

> "So, are you saying that you first added the tens together? And then you added the ones?"

→ **Present an organizational frame.** Create a graphic organizer or anchor chart or simply rely on your prior teaching to help the student organize what she has to say.

> "Where will your story take place? What will happen first? What will happen next?"

→ **Arrange for a do-over later.** If you feel you cannot publicly and quickly get the student back on track, plan to help him individually and give him a chance to present again later.

> "Ken, I'm intrigued by what you're saying, but I want to make sure everyone understands your main point. Let's talk in a few minutes, and then you can present again after lunch."

Essential Skills at a Glance

CRAFTING AN ARGUMENT	
Speaking in an Organized Way (pages 107–113)	→ When describing a person, place, thing, or experience, state the main topic and add the most important and interesting details. → When appropriate, recount a story, event, or process in a sequential or logical way.
Distinguishing Facts From Opinions (pages 113–118)	→ Know what's a fact and what's an opinion. → Present facts in a way that tells listeners the information can be verified. → Present opinions in a way that tells listeners these are the speaker's personal beliefs.
Presenting Evidence (pages 119–122)	→ Cite relevant facts, evidence, and reasons to support opinions. → Know what kinds of evidence tends to be most effective.
Persuading Others (pages 122–124)	→ Begin by stating the main idea or position. → Provide reasons and evidence to support the main idea and any opinions. → Use an appropriate tone of voice. Be assertive, but respectful. → Avoid overselling or being too argumentative.

Sample Letter to Parents

Dear Parents,

We're starting to go even deeper with children's conversation skills. In the coming weeks, we'll be working on organizing our ideas, differentiating between facts and opinions, and backing up what we have to say with evidence.

As always, I want to share a few simple ideas for practicing these skills at home:

- Help your child recount events in order. For example, when she or he retells a family event, encourage her or him to go in order: "What happened first? Then what happened?" Helping children organize their speaking will also help them develop the systematic thinking skills they need in all academic subject areas.

- Give your child positive feedback when he or she puts these skills to use. To give you an idea how this works, when a child relates a home event to me, I might say, "Wow, you told me that story in such a clear way, I feel like I really know what happened. You started at the beginning and then chose a few key details to flesh out the story."

- View media together and talk about these skills. For instance, "Is what that TV reporter said a fact or an opinion? Does this blog post make sense to you?"

As always, please let me know if you have any questions or thoughts. Thank you for supporting your child's learning!

The Art of Agreeing and Disagreeing

Respectful, Collaborative, Productive

When children actively learn from their classmates, they can maximize their understanding. And in order to learn from one another at a deep, meaningful level, they need to know how to respectfully agree and disagree. The more students learn to grapple with one another's ideas—and still maintain positive relationships—the more successful they'll also be as friends, co-workers, family members, and citizens of a democracy.

This fourth grade social studies lesson shows how powerful a respectful exchange of ideas in classroom conversations can be. The teacher, Mrs. Rodriguez, begins by presenting the debate topic, pros and cons of the First Amendment's free speech guarantee: "The framers of our Constitution decided to include a right to free speech, to say and publish what you want. Is this still a good idea?" She then encourages students to back up their opinions with reasons and evidence.

CHAPTER 5

Common Core Connections · · · · · 137

How to Teach the Skills:

   Agreeing · · · · · · · · · · · · · · · 141

   Disagreeing · · · · · · · · · · · · · 148

   Partially Agreeing · · · · · · · · · 155

   Responding to Disagreements · · 157

Giving Meaningful Feedback · · · 162

Addressing Common Mistakes · · 165

Essential Skills at a Glance · · · · · 168

Sample Letter to Parents · · · · · · 169

Cleo starts, "We need free speech. I read in our textbook that if we didn't have it, you could get in trouble for saying certain things, like you think the government is wrong." Nora nods and says, "I agree, and I want to add a different reason. I read that free speech also means I can say, 'I think so-and-so isn't a good singer,' and he can't sue me or anything."

Many children nod, and Assad adds, "If we didn't have free speech and you couldn't say that he isn't a good singer, people might buy his music and waste their money." Alexa quietly chimes in, "I mostly agree, but I worry when people say things that aren't true. Sometimes people lie and lots of people will still believe them, but then no one listens when the real story comes out."

The conversation continues with more students agreeing, adding new points, partially agreeing, or disagreeing. By learning to exchange ideas, these students are able to wrestle with challenging questions while maintaining positive relationships with each other and keeping open minds—something that even adults often find hard to do.

In this chapter, you'll learn how to boost students' proficiency in the art of agreeing and disagreeing. You'll also gather practical ideas for teaching these skills in ways that inspire students to engage in deep and meaningful learning conversations.

Why These Skills Matter

Thoughtful exchanges of ideas and opinions are an integral part of students' academic and social learning because they:

→ **Deepen students' understanding.** When students hear additional ideas and conflicting views and take that new information into account, they often learn at a higher level. In literature discussions, they can gain a greater appreciation of plot and character; in math, they can learn to solve problems in new and different ways; in science, they can grapple with making sense of the varied results from an experiment; and in social studies, they can better understand multiple points of view on historic events.

→ **Lead to higher-level critical thinking skills.** Deciding whether they agree or disagree with a statement and examining the validity of a classmate's evidence require students to think critically. This kind of thinking is crucial for lifelong learning—to understand complex texts, think through challenging math and science problems, analyze historical and current events, and thoughtfully evaluate a work of art or musical composition.

→ **Prepare students for "real life" conversations.** In social and work situations, people have to participate in conversations about complicated issues and make decisions based on multilayered, even conflicting, information while maintaining collegial relationships. The skills in this chapter will prepare students for that challenge.

Common Core Connections

Kindergarten

SL.K.1: Participate in collaborative conversations with diverse partners about kindergarten topics and texts.

SL.K.1a: Follow agreed-upon rules for discussions.

SL.K.1b: Continue a conversation through multiple exchanges.

SL.K.6: Speak audibly and express thoughts, feelings, and ideas clearly.

1st Grade

SL.1.1: Participate in collaborative conversations with diverse partners about grade 1 topics and texts.

SL.1.1a: Follow agreed-upon rules for discussions.

SL.1.1b: Build on others' talk in conversations.

SL.1.4: Describe people, places, things, and events with relevant details, expressing ideas and feelings clearly.

SL.1.6: Produce complete sentences when appropriate to task and situation.

2nd Grade

SL.2.1: Participate in collaborative conversations with diverse partners about grade 2 topics and texts.

SL.2.1a: Follow agreed-upon rules for discussions.

SL.2.1b: Build on others' talk in conversations by linking their comments to the remarks of others.

SL.2.4: Tell a story or recount an experience with appropriate facts and relevant, descriptive details, speaking audibly in coherent sentences.

SL.2.6: Produce complete sentences when appropriate to task and situation in order to provide requested detail or clarification.

3rd Grade

SL.3.1: Engage effectively in a range of collaborative discussions (one-on-one, in groups, and teacher-led) with diverse partners on grade 3 topics and texts.

SL.3.1a: Come to discussions prepared.

SL.3.1b: Follow agreed-upon rules for discussions.

SL.3.1c: Link comments to the remarks of others.

SL.3.1d: Explain ideas and understanding in light of the discussion.

SL.3.4: Report on a topic or text, tell a story, or recount an experience with appropriate facts and relevant, descriptive details, speaking clearly at an understandable pace.

SL.3.6: Speak in complete sentences when appropriate to task and situation.

4th Grade

SL.4.1: Engage effectively in a range of collaborative discussions (one-on-one, in groups, and teacher-led) with diverse partners on grade 4 topics and texts.

SL.4.1a: Come to discussions prepared.

SL.4.1b: Follow agreed-upon rules for discussions.

SL.4.1c. Pose and respond to specific questions to clarify or follow up on information, and make comments that contribute to the discussion and link to the remarks of others.

SL.4.1d. Review the key ideas expressed and explain ideas and understanding in light of the discussion.

SL.4.4: Report on a topic or text, tell a story, or recount an experience in an organized manner, using appropriate facts and relevant, descriptive details to support main ideas or themes; speak clearly at an understandable pace.

SL.4.6: Differentiate between contexts that call for formal English and situations where informal discourse is appropriate; use formal English when appropriate to task and situation.

5th Grade

SL.5.1: Engage effectively in a range of collaborative discussions (one-on-one, in groups, and teacher-led) with diverse partners on grade 5 topics and texts.

5th Grade, cont.

SL.5.1a: Come to discussions prepared.

SL.5.1b: Follow agreed-upon rules for discussions.

SL.5.1c: Make comments that contribute to the discussion and elaborate on the remarks of others.

SL.5.1d: Review the key ideas expressed and draw conclusions in light of information and knowledge gained from the discussions.

SL.5.3: Summarize the points a speaker makes and explain how each claim is supported by reasons and evidence.

SL.5.4: Report on a topic or text or present an opinion, sequencing ideas logically and using appropriate facts and relevant, descriptive details to support main ideas or themes; speak clearly at an understandable pace.

SL.5.6: Adapt speech to a variety of contexts and tasks, using formal English when appropriate to task and situation.

6th Grade

SL.6.1: Engage effectively in a range of collaborative discussions (one-on-one, in groups, and teacher-led) with diverse partners on grade 6 topics and texts.

SL.6.1a: Come to discussions prepared.

SL.6.1b: Follow rules for collegial discussions.

SL.6.1c: Make comments that contribute to the topic, text, or issue under discussion.

SL.6.1d: Review the key ideas expressed and demonstrate understanding of multiple perspectives.

SL.6.3: Delineate a speaker's argument and specific claims, distinguishing claims that are supported by reasons and evidence from claims that are not.

SL.6.4: Present claims and findings, sequencing ideas logically and using pertinent descriptions, facts, and details to accentuate main ideas or themes; use appropriate eye contact, adequate volume, and clear pronunciation.

SL.6.6: Adapt speech to a variety of contexts and tasks, demonstrating command of formal English when indicated or appropriate.

How to Teach the Skills

Here are some tips for success when teaching the art of agreeing and disagreeing:

→ **Show empathy.** The skills this chapter covers are challenging, so offer your understanding and support if students struggle with them. You can still provide constructive feedback when needed, but remember to do so with a patient tone that does not shut students down.

→ **Pose open-ended questions.** When students deal with questions that have no definitive answer, they're more likely to take risks by offering their opinions and trying to back up their positions with reasons and evidence. Compared with closed-ended questions, open-ended questions present more opportunities for students to agree, elaborate, disagree, and challenge.

→ **Teach one skill at a time.** This way, students can better grasp the nuances of each skill and develop their abilities to put it to use. As students begin to show fluency, introduce the next skill, being sure to provide opportunities to practice the skills in combination.

→ **Consider students' developmental needs.** Children in certain grades may find the skills in this chapter especially challenging. For instance, fifth and sixth graders tend to be very conscious of what their peers think of them and deeply concerned with issues of fairness. These students will enjoy serious discussions and debates, but they'll likely also need extra practice and support in engaging respectfully and considering their classmates' feelings, especially when expressing disagreement.

Core skills for agreeing and disagreeing

✓ **Agreeing thoughtfully**

✓ **Disagreeing respectfully**

✓ **Expressing partial agreement**

✓ **Responding to disagreements**

→ **Keep in mind children's cultural backgrounds.** Some of the skills in this chapter, especially publicly disagreeing with another person, might conflict with a child's home culture. Remember to explain that these skills can support success in school, college, and the workplace, and to show respect for the child's home culture.

On the following pages, you'll learn practical ways to teach the art of agreeing and disagreeing in the natural course of the school day, both by offering separate lessons and by weaving this teaching into your academic lessons.

For a suggested timeline of when to teach academic conversation skills throughout the school year, see page 191.

AGREEING THOUGHTFULLY

Students need to learn how to make positive connections to others' comments—connections that are truly meaningful, advance the conversation, and deepen everyone's understanding. Specifically, students need to know how to provide reasons and evidence for why they agree, and also how to add on to others' ideas.

Providing Reasons and Evidence for Agreeing

For younger students, who have less experience with the art of conversation and need a concrete presentation of how to agree, I find Interactive Modeling (page 172) to be the most straightforward approach to use. Here's how you might do the lesson in the context of a conversation about books:

→ **State how agreeing can help them learn.**

> "In our book conversations, we sometimes need to let the speaker know when we agree with something she said and why. Explaining why we agree helps keep the conversation going and helps everyone understand what the speaker said. See what you notice about how I agree with something Anjali says about our book."

→ **Briefly demonstrate thoughtful agreement.** For example, suppose Anjali gave her opinion about a character from the book *Swimmy* by Leo Lionni: "I think Swimmy was brave because he swam in the ocean on his own." Show how to agree with the statement while explaining why:

"I agree with you, Anjali, because it must have been scary to see all those different creatures and be surrounded by so much water with no place to hide."

→ **Ask students what they noticed about how you agreed.** Be sure they point out that you gave two reasons for why you agreed. If students don't notice on their own, you may also want to tell them that agreements should contribute to the conversation—in other words, make it more interesting and more helpful to everyone.

→ **Let students practice agreeing.** Using the same book or a different one, state an opinion about a character or scene that students are likely to agree with, but one that's rich enough for them to be able to offer different reasons for agreeing with your ideas. For example: "Swimmy's most helpful idea was arranging the small fish into a big fish." Let students practice offering some agreement statements with partners first and then with the whole group. You may also want to use anchor charts or sentence stems to help students with the language of agreeing (see pages 144–145).

For older students, who generally have more experience with classroom conversations, you may want to introduce the skill with a Fishbowl demonstration (page 174). Here's how one sixth grade teacher used the Fishbowl with her students during a civics lesson:

→ **Prepare the student demonstrators in advance.** The day before, this teacher told the students who were going to be in the Fishbowl that they would be discussing whether the federal government reflects "a true representative democracy." She had them practice ways to agree with one another's assertions.

→ **Prepare the observers.** Just before the demonstration, she prompted those observing the Fishbowl discussion to pay particular attention to when speakers agreed with others and how that agreement helped the conversation.

→ **Set a time limit for the discussion.** The students in the Fishbowl had a brief, lively discussion that included several exchanges in which students agreed with one another. For example:

Darryl: "I'm not sure Congress is really democratic because I read in our textbook that states arrange it so that only certain people can get elected."

Elena: "I agree with Darryl. It doesn't seem fair to divide up a state so that some places have mostly all Republican voters or all Democratic voters. Then your representative won't have to listen to you if you're not from the same party."

→ **Debrief together.** After the teacher signals for the discussion to end, she asks observers what they noticed. Here are two of their observations:

- The speakers who agreed contributed to the conversation. It sounded like they wanted to learn more, not just talk for the sake of talking.

- The speakers gave specific reasons and evidence for why they agreed.

→ **Give students a chance to practice the skill right away.** The teacher has students talk with partners, using Darryl's statement as the starting point. She reminds them to limit their discussion to why they agree with his statement. She lets them know they'll have opportunities outside of this practice to express any disagreement.

→ **Have students reflect.** After students have had a chance to practice, the teacher asks them to think about how expressing agreement contributes to conversations.

"How can agreeing the way we've been practicing help us in our future conversations?"

Students note that when people are agreeing, they're often giving different reasons and additional evidence. They also notice that hearing these different reasons helps some "undecided" listeners figure out whether they also agree.

Practice the skill. After your initial teaching, give students opportunities to practice thoughtful agreement. Remind students that for the purposes of learning this skill, conversations should focus on reasons and evidence for agreeing. Here are some ways to incorporate this practice into your academic teaching:

➜ **Use practice structures such as Inside-Outside Circles or Maître d'** (page 180) to enable students to talk with a series of partners or groups. For each round, give students a position on an engaging topic. For instance, with younger students you might say, "Weather is sometimes harmful to people"; with older students, "It would be great if humans could control the weather." Have students brainstorm all the reasons they might agree with your statement and let them practice expressing that agreement in meaningful ways.

➜ **Play Four Corners** with students (page 178). Give the class a question with four answer options. For instance, you might ask, "On the basis of what we've studied, which of these animals do you think has adapted best to its environment—ants, snakes, chameleons, or gophers?" Students go to the corner that represents the animal they choose. With a partner or the whole group in that corner, have students brainstorm all the reasons they agree on that animal.

➜ **Practice the skills during morning meetings and closing circles.** For instance, you might have students share on an opinion-based topic, such as a law that students would like to see changed or one thing they wish were different about the world. After a student shares, give other students a chance to agree in the same ways you've taught.

Provide ongoing support. As students put the skills of agreeing to use:

➜ **Post anchor charts.** Later, as you teach more agreement skills, you might want to add ideas to these charts.

> **How to Agree Thoughtfully**
> * Say why you agree.
> * Give a reason or evidence.
> * Be brief.

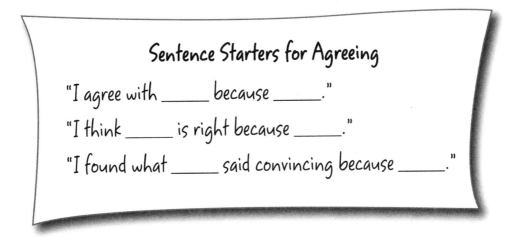

Sentence Starters for Agreeing

"I agree with _____ because _____."

"I think _____ is right because _____."

"I found what _____ said convincing because _____."

→ **Give reminders.** Before sending students off for small-group conversations or holding a whole-group discussion, remind them what they've learned about agreement.

> "Who can remind us of how we can agree as people share their opinions?"

→ **Use partner chats before having whole-class discussions.** Occasionally, have students practice meaningful agreement with partners first before doing so as part of the whole group. The chats will help them remember to make connections to what others are saying.

Adding On to Others' Ideas

Introduce the skill. For academic conversations to deepen understanding, students must know when and how to elaborate on someone else's statement by adding new information, new reasons, or new evidence. Building up the conversation this way provides everyone with greater insights into a topic and a greater appreciation for multiple points of view.

In the following example, a second grade teacher, Ms. Johnson, taught her students how to add on to, or "piggyback" on, someone else's comment during a science lesson. Ms. Johnson asked some fourth graders to serve as demonstrators for an Expert Demonstration; see page 175. (If you teach older students, you can adapt this lesson as a Fishbowl demonstration; see page 174.) Here are the key steps in Ms. Johnson's Expert Demonstration:

→ **Set students up for success** by briefly telling them the learning purpose.

> "Sometimes in our conversations, we want to add on to what another person said. We might do this to give more details or ideas. Watch and listen to how the fourth graders discuss the passage we read about germs."

→ **Prepare the expert demonstrators in advance.** Ms. Johnson invited fourth graders who were experienced with this conversation skill to demonstrate. She had them read the same text passage about germs that the second graders had read.

→ **Remind the class to watch closely** to see the skill in action. Here's an example of how these fourth graders added on to one another's comments:

Cyrus: "When people say 'germs,' those can be either bacteria or viruses."

Clara: "I want to add two more—protozoa or fungi."

Cyrus: "Oh, I forgot those."

Reed: "It also said in the book that even though some people think all germs are bad, sometimes germs do good things."

Cyrus: "Yes, I read that some bacteria live in our intestines and help us digest our food."

Clara: "And scientists sometimes use bacteria and fungi to make vaccines or do experiments, so that's another reason they are not bad."

→ **Guide the class in reflecting on the demonstration.** Ms. Johnson asked her students what they noticed about how the demonstrators elaborated on others' ideas. Her students noticed that:

- The demonstrators added facts—evidence from the text—that helped them cover everything they read in the passage.

- What they added connected to what the person before had said.

- They were respectful. They didn't put people down or tell them that they had messed up.

→ **Have the class practice right after the demonstration.** Next, Ms. Johnson's class discussed the same text in small groups. They focused on adding on to what was said, while she circulated and coached them—and gave positive feedback (see pages 162–164).

Practice the skill in all subject areas. Students may especially enjoy learning the skill (and using the term) of "piggybacking" and catch on to it relatively quickly. To truly master this skill, however, it's important that students use it frequently in all subject areas.

→ **Use partner chats first.** Assign student pairs a task such as remembering key facts from a text, reviewing steps they took in a science experiment, or brainstorming adjectives to describe a book character. Encourage students to use specific language to add on to what their partner said. You may want to refer them to an anchor chart, such as the one shown. Then point out when students use these phrases:

> **Adding On**
>
> "Also, I read that _____."
>
> "In addition to what you said, I remember that _____."
>
> "I want to piggyback on what _____ said by adding _____."

> "I heard people use words like 'also,' 'in addition,' 'I want to piggyback on,' and 'I have another reason.' Those words signal to others in a conversation that you're staying on the same topic but just adding more information."

→ **Next, have students talk in small groups.** Once students have become fairly adept at adding on with a partner, have them practice in small groups. For instance, as students discuss a book they read, remind them to elaborate on what someone else said:

> "As you discuss your books, remember to add on to the reasons or evidence someone else gives, as we've been practicing. That way, your group can flesh out the ideas you're talking about."

→ **Encourage students to use the skill during whole-group discussions.** For example, if you called a class meeting to discuss problems children are having at recess, ask one student to describe the situation. Then invite others to elaborate on what that student shared to make sure everyone has a clear understanding of what's happening before moving on to discuss possible solutions.

Provide ongoing support:

→ **Use anchor charts** to give students general guidelines for when to add on. As students develop greater expertise, add additional guidelines to the chart. See a sample chart for students just beginning to learn this skill at right:

→ **Model the skill yourself.** From time to time, point out when you use the skill of adding on. The more expert modeling students see, the better they'll get at adding on in ways that advance academic conversations.

When to Add On

* Add a reason you think is missing.

* Add more facts you think are important.

* Add an idea that will help everyone understand someone else's idea.

DISAGREEING RESPECTFULLY

Once students learn how to agree meaningfully with each other, they'll be ready to move on to the more nuanced skill of disagreeing respectfully. Students need to learn that conversations are most productive when speakers can express honest and well-founded disagreements and question statements they're not sure about in ways that preserve relationships.

This means pausing and evaluating another speaker's statement first, rather than immediately disagreeing or taking sides. Then, if students do disagree, it means respectfully providing reasons and evidence for their disagreement and courteously challenging someone else's reasons and evidence.

Giving Reasons and Evidence for Disagreeing

Introduce the skill. Many children have internalized adults' well-meant message that being kind and polite means they should not show disagreement. Talk with your students about the benefits of respectful disagreement.

> "We've been working on having meaningful conversations to help us learn. Sometimes we might disagree with our classmates. Why might it be helpful for us to tell each other when we disagree?"

If students have studied historic figures who have expressed disagreement, such as Rosa Parks or Mahatma Gandhi, point to their work as examples of the importance of voicing disagreement. Be direct when you conclude this discussion:

> "So in our class, it's OK to disagree. But we need to express our disagreement respectfully."

Then you can use an Interactive Modeling lesson (page 172) to introduce the skill of disagreeing honestly and respectfully. You could do this in the context of a discussion about solving a math problem that has multiple solutions.

→ **Say what you will model and why:**

> "I'll show you how to disagree in a way that is both respectful and informative. Watch how I disagree with Solange about a math problem."

→ **Demonstrate respectful disagreement.** Have a student explain her solution to a math problem and why it's the only solution. Then show how to use your voice and body language to disagree respectfully. Also be sure to model giving a sound reason for your disagreement:

> "Solange, I respectfully disagree that your solution is the only one. I think there is another way to join the four triangles and make a new shape. May I show you?"

➤ **Guide students in pointing out key aspects of your demonstration.** You may want to prompt students with a question:

> "How did I show Solange that I disagreed while still making sure to treat her kindly and respectfully?"

Encourage children to notice your courteous tone of voice, kind facial expression, friendly body language, and the words you chose. Then ask a follow-up question to promote greater understanding:

> "How did my disagreement help everyone's learning?"

Students might point out that you provided a reason for your disagreement and helped everyone see a new way to solve the problem.

➤ **Give students an immediate chance to practice.** Using a similar math problem, pair students up and have them practice expressing disagreement and the reasons behind it the same way you modeled.

Practice the skill. One lesson and practice session will not be enough for students to learn this skill, so give them multiple opportunities to practice. Here are some ideas for productive practice sessions.

➤ **Use Venn diagrams.** Some children need time to feel comfortable with disagreeing, so providing structure by way of Venn diagrams can feel less charged.

- *Pair students up* and give each a blank Venn diagram. Have one partner put his name in the left circle, the other in the right, and label the middle area as "both."

- *Give students a series of opinion statements* based on the work they've been doing. These examples are from a unit on environmental science:

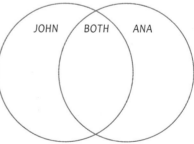

Styrofoam should be banned.
People should eat less meat.
Showers should be shorter than five minutes.

- *If both students agree with a statement,* they write it in the "both" area. If only one person agrees, he writes it in his circle. If neither agrees, the statement goes on the outside of the Venn diagram.

- *Encourage students to back up their choices* by briefly discussing their reasons for agreeing or disagreeing with each other. As an extension, you may want to have two pairs combine into a small group and compare diagrams while practicing respectfully offering reasons and evidence for why they disagree with another's opinion.

- *Give students positive feedback* when you see them using what they learned about disagreeing:

> "I hear many of you respectfully telling your partners why you don't agree with the other person's position. You're also giving valid evidence to back up what you say."

→ **Make the practice engaging.** For instance, at morning meetings or other class gatherings, you could play games like This, That, Neither, Both (page 185):

- *Have students stand in a circle.* Place a rope or long strip of tape down the center of the circle.

- *Read two opinion statements.* For younger students, keep these simple: "Dogs make great pets" and "Cats make great pets." For older students, you can use more involved academic topics: "The right to free speech is the most important of the Bill of Rights" and "The freedom from unreasonable searches and seizures is the most important of the Bill of Rights." Designate one half of the circle to represent one opinion, the other half to represent the other opinion.

- *Signal students to move.* If they agree with both statements, they stand in the middle of the circle. If they agree with only one statement, they move to the appropriate half of the circle. If they disagree with both statements, they move outside the circle.

- *Tell students to find a partner* who made the same choice they did. Have them brainstorm as many reasons and facts as they can to support their choice.

- *Call on a few students* to share the reasons and evidence for their views. Let students move to a new area if they were persuaded to change their opinions.

→ **Remind students to put the skills to use** before they embark on small-group discussions or projects:

> "As your group works on finding as many different solutions as possible to our geometry challenge, what do you need to remember about how to agree and disagree respectfully?"

Provide ongoing support. As children learn to disagree respectfully, they'll need frequent feedback, coaching, and encouragement.

→ **Create anchor charts** like the ones shown, or add to existing ones. These can be especially helpful to students who are struggling with this skill. You can either create these charts yourself and teach the content to students or engage students in helping you generate the content.

How to Disagree Respectfully
* Use a polite tone.
* State a different opinion.
* Give a reason or fact.

→ **Use individual or small-group practice** to provide extra help for students whose disagreements too often come out sounding confrontational or demeaning. They may feel passionate about certain topics, but need more practice learning how to express strong views in ways that respect people's feelings. From time to time, sit with these students and coach them as they participate in various classroom discussions.

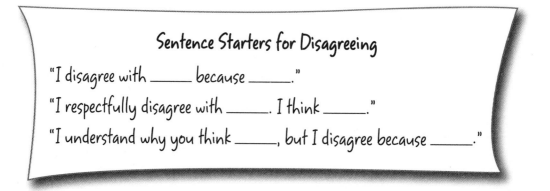

Sentence Starters for Disagreeing

"I disagree with _____ because _____."

"I respectfully disagree with _____. I think _____."

"I understand why you think _____, but I disagree because _____."

Questioning Someone's Reasons and Evidence

Introduce the skill. Students also need to know how to challenge someone's statement respectfully if they think it's incorrect or based on flawed reasoning. Remind students to wait before asserting a challenge because they need to give themselves time to consider exactly why they're questioning what someone said. You can use Interactive Modeling (page 172) to do this teaching.

→ **State why this skill is important:**

> "We all sometimes make mistakes in conversations. Maybe we have our facts wrong; maybe we make an argument that's not logical. When someone does that, we can help them uncover the mistake and learn from it. Watch and see how that looks in my conversation with Hildy."

→ **Demonstrate respectfully challenging someone.** Prepare a student in advance to make a mistake in speaking—one that's not too obvious. For instance, she might say, "Spiders are insects because they have a head and a thorax, just like insects do." Then show students that you're carefully considering what the student said before you reply, "Hmm, I thought to be an insect, a creature had to have six legs, but a spider has eight. Let's check our book to find out."

→ **Guide students to point out key aspects** of questioning someone's reasons or evidence.

> "How did I question what Hildy said while still being kind and respectful?"

Be sure students notice the friendly tone of voice you used, how you started with "Hmm, I thought," not a statement like "You're wrong!" and how you used facts to back up what you had to say.

→ **Present students with an inaccurate statement** and let them practice challenging it. For instance, you might use a similar science example: "A millipede is an insect because it has a hard exoskeleton. It molts, and when it's frightened, it curls up into a ball."

Practice the skill. Challenging someone's statement is one of the hardest skills for students to learn, so be sure to give them multiple chances to practice in safe contexts.

→ **Use Swap Meet** (page 184). Present students with a flawed statement, such as a math solution that contains errors. Students then discuss in pairs how they would respectfully challenge your statement. Next let a few students share out their ideas. Then have students swap partners and repeat, giving them a new flawed statement. Highlight what students do well each time:

> "You pointed out that my estimate was based on an incomplete set of data. You did that in a way that made me feel like you were helping me, not attacking me."

→ **Give students a heads-up** when they may need to use the skill of challenging someone's statement in an upcoming activity. This also lets students who'll be speaking know to anticipate some challenges. For instance, when students are presenting findings from science experiments, you might say:

> "Who can remind us what to do if we think there's an error or problem with a classmate's work?"

Provide ongoing support. As students start to develop this skill, be patient, give regular feedback and coaching, and provide concrete supports.

→ **Post anchor charts,** such as the ones on the next page, and refer to them before students encounter situations where they may need to challenge a statement. Add to these charts as students make progress or as you discover what reminders they most need.

→ **Provide extra help for students who challenge too much.** Some students may be adept "challengers," questioning assertions so frequently that other students feel attacked. Eventually, classmates may start to ostracize them. Help these students by coaching them individually. Decide together on a limit for challenges (such as three per day or seven per week). You might also practice one-on-one with the student, focusing on how to pause and think before making a challenge.

How to Challenge Respectfully

* Challenge speakers only on important issues.
* Speak politely.
* Offer valid reasons and evidence.

Challenging Someone's Assertions

"I think you might have made a mistake because _____."

"I don't understand how you _____ because _____."

"Something doesn't seem quite right. Would you please explain more about _____?"

EXPRESSING PARTIAL AGREEMENT

Once students become proficient with agreeing and disagreeing, you can teach them how to express partial agreement. Make sure students still understand the benefits of expressing when they agree with some parts of what someone said, even if they disagree with other parts.

Introduce the skill. You can use an Interactive Modeling lesson (page 172) to teach students how to express partial agreement.

➔ **Set the stage for your modeling:**

"We've been learning how to agree and disagree, but what should we do if we both agree and disagree at the same time? I'm going to show you how this looks and sounds. See what you notice."

→ **Provide a clear model.** When you model partial agreement, be sure to use explicit language about the parts of a statement you agree with and those you disagree with.

> "I agree with Kim that all squares are rectangles, but I disagree with the part when she said all rectangles are square. To be square, each side has to be the same length, but some rectangles have short sides and long sides."

Practice the skill. Deciding which parts of a statement one agrees with and which parts one disagrees with requires analytical thinking first. Then, to express those thoughts well, requires speaking clearly and using precise wording. Give students many chances to practice this "think-first-then-speak" combination. Here are some ideas to try:

→ **Use partner practice structures such as Inside-Outside Circles** (page 180) or simple partner chats. Give students statements that are likely to elicit simultaneous agreement and disagreement. For example, "Goldilocks was a bad person because she broke the rules and didn't listen to her mother." Or "Plants need sunlight and water, but they also need human contact to thrive." Let partners practice how they would express their partial agreement. Then let some students share out to the class.

→ **Use small groups.** For instance, give each group a math problem and one solution to analyze. Let students in the group discuss which steps of the solution they think are mathematically sound and which they think are questionable.

Provide ongoing support. As students practice and use this skill of simultaneously agreeing and disagreeing in conversations, try these ideas for promoting their progress:

→ **Post anchor charts or sentence starters** (like the one on the opposite page). Often students simply need help getting started. Sentence starters can help them clarify their thinking and articulate their positions so that others can understand why they agree and disagree.

When You Partially Agree

"I sort of agree with _____. I agree that _____, but I think that _____."

"I think _____ is right that _____, but I also think that _____."

"I agree with _____, but I disagree with _____."

→ **Paraphrase what students say.** Sometimes you may notice a student struggling with getting her ideas out and be concerned that she'll get too discouraged if she has to keep restating her ideas. In situations like this, you might want to step in and paraphrase, serving as a model for her for next time.

> "So, it sounds as if you agree with Anju that snakes are sometimes deadly, but you disagree that gopher snakes, the example she used, fall in that category. Is that right?"

RESPONDING TO DISAGREEMENTS

The next step for students in their quest to build strong classroom conversations is learning how to respond when someone disagrees with them. This skill can be very challenging, especially for younger students, but it's a critical one to devote time to because of its potential for deepening academic discussions and ensuring a positive learning community.

This is a complex skill set—requiring students to know their options for responding, quickly choosing their best option, and then expressing that option appropriately. It's best to teach these steps all at once because when someone disagrees, the speaker needs to be able to use the skills together to keep the conversation—and the learning—moving forward.

For older students, you can introduce these skills using the following modified version of Interactive Modeling (page 172):

➙ **Brainstorm options for responding.** Present the class with a situation.

> "In a conversation, when someone disagrees with or challenges my position, I have several choices. For instance, I could decide that what I said was correct and defend it with additional reasons. What else could I do?"

➙ **Use students' responses to create an anchor chart.** Coach them as needed to ensure that the key ideas shown below are included on the chart:

When someone disagrees with you, you can:

* Admit you might be wrong.

* Change your position and explain why.

* Stick with your position and provide additional reasons and evidence to back it up.

* Say nothing and keep listening to learn what others have to say.

➙ **Prepare the class for your modeling:**

> "Now let's see what it looks like when I choose one of these options. Watch and see what you notice."

➙ **Demonstrate the skill with a volunteer.** For example:

Teacher: "I solved the math problem of how many oranges we would need for everyone to have six ounces of juice. The book said you can squeeze about 2 ounces of juice from every orange. I figured each of us needs three oranges, and because there are 21 of us, I counted by 3's and got 62."

The student volunteer might say: "I think something might be off with your counting, because I multiplied 3 times 21 and got 63."

Pause and then respond by demonstrating one of the strategies: "I wonder if you're right. Maybe we should try it together."

↪ **Have students point out key aspects of what you did.** For instance, be sure students notice that you did not get upset or insist that you were right, and that because you weren't sure of the correct answer, you planned to do more investigating.

↪ **Let students do a quick practice.** Give students a chance to discuss with partners how they have solved related math problems. Prompt them to put these responding skills to use if a classmate disagrees with them.

Given how complex responding to disagreements is, you may want to do additional lessons, focusing on each of the other options. Or using the anchor chart from the previous page, have students do a Fishbowl demonstration (page 174) in which they can choose any of the options. Over time, they should try to use all the responding skills you taught in your initial lesson.

For younger students, begin with a much narrower range of options modifying the lesson above. For instance:

> "When someone disagrees with you in a conversation, you have three choices—to acknowledge the disagreement (that is, say nothing, nod, and keep listening), to agree, or to disagree."

You could then practice what each option looks and sounds like, referring back to the earlier teaching you had done about agreeing and disagreeing.

Practice the skill. Give students regular opportunities to practice the skills of responding to disagreements.

↪ **Paired Verbal Fluency** (page 182) is an especially powerful technique for practicing how to respond to someone else's comments. Here's one way to use this technique to focus on these skills:

• Place students in pairs. One is A, the other is B.

- Provide an interesting topic for discussion. For instance, younger students could discuss "What really happened at the end of *I Want My Hat Back*?" For older students: "Do you think *Wonder* was realistic?"

- A goes first. She gives her position on the topic for one minute. B then has one minute to express his opinions. During that time, he may decide to disagree with something A said.

- Give each student 30 more seconds to respond to what the other person has said, including responding to any disagreements. To conclude, each student has 20 additional seconds to make his or her last point.

→ **Pros and Cons** (page 183) can be especially useful if you think students might get too emotional as they practice. That's because students are assigned a position to argue. When they're less personally attached, they can practice responding to disagreements in a more detached way.

- Place students in pairs. Assign one to be "pro" and the other "con."

- Give all students the same controversial statement related to a topic they're studying, for instance: "We should have laws banning the sale of soda pop to anyone under 18." Students then have two minutes to think up (and list, if helpful) as many reasons as possible to support their assigned position.

- The "pro" students present some of their reasons to their partner for one minute. Then, the "con" students present some of their reasons for one minute.

- Students take turns challenging one of their partner's statements and allowing their partner to respond. Allow a few rounds of this back-and-forth while you observe and provide coaching and feedback.

Provide ongoing support. The ability to respond effectively when someone disagrees with you is essential to analyzing problems and thinking critically. For younger students especially, you may want to do more one-on-one or small-group practice than usual because of the complexity of this skill, and some older students will likely need extra practice as well. To make the most of these practices:

→ **Remind students frequently.** Before conversations you know might be tricky or highly charged, remind students of the expectations and ask them what they'll need to do to be successful. Occasionally refer them to the "When someone disagrees with you" anchor chart (page 158) as a reminder of respectful options when others disagree with their position.

→ **Provide sentence starters** for responding to disagreements. Add to these as students show readiness for more nuanced responses or if you discover they need more support with certain skills.

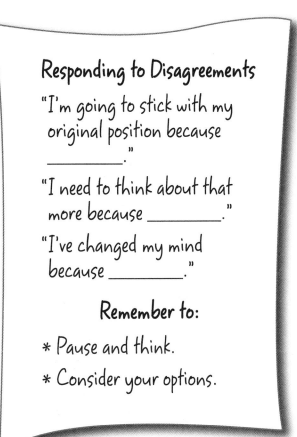

Responding to Disagreements

"I'm going to stick with my original position because _____."

"I need to think about that more because _____."

"I've changed my mind because _____."

Remember to:

* Pause and think.

* Consider your options.

Giving Meaningful Feedback

As students learn the skills outlined in this chapter, one of the most powerful ways you can support their growth is through positive reinforcement. As often as you can, encourage students—point out what they're doing well so they can build on their successes and ultimately master these important skills.

LOOK FOR PROGRESS, NOT PERFECTION

Rather than expecting (or hoping for) perfection, look for small steps in the right direction.

→ **Point out successes in using reasons or evidence**. For example, when a student provides additional evidence for her position (even if her tone is not ideal), you might say:

> "Kourtney, I noticed you backed up your disagreement with Scott by referring to the text. When you use evidence like that, it helps everyone reconsider their positions."

→ **Point out successes in being respectful.** Even if the reasons and evidence students provide are not that strong, give them positive feedback when they remember to use the respectful language or tone you taught them. For example:

> "You've all been remembering to use the phrases 'I agree' or 'I respectfully disagree' to start your statements. That gives your listeners a clue about what you're going to say and helps prepare them to follow along with your thinking."

→ **Avoid pointing out a mistake right after giving positive feedback.** Find another time to address the mistake. Otherwise, your positive feedback will lose its power. See Chapter 2, page 62, for more on this technique.

HELP STUDENTS SEE THE POWER OF AGREEING AND DISAGREEING

While students are learning the skills of agreeing, disagreeing, and responding to disagreements, they may lose sight of the bigger picture—that everyone learns more when ideas are exchanged. As you give students positive feedback, point out from time to time why their success matters:

→ **Connect to their learning.** Whenever possible, tell the whole class how their exchange of ideas advanced everyone's understanding of a text or concept.

> "Look what a difference all of our brains have made! At first we each thought of only one way to build a tower from paper and tape. Now that we've combined our ideas, our structure is stronger."

→ **Point out open-mindedness in thinking.** Students need to see the benefits of being flexible in their thinking after receiving more information.

> "During our conversation, many of you were willing to consider the new information and ideas they heard. Some of you changed your opinions based on what others said. That kind of flexibility helps you think like scientists."

TIME YOUR FEEDBACK
FOR GREATEST EFFECT

As your students' conversations become richer and deeper, your best teaching stance is that of facilitator—helping to keep the conversation moving forward, not controlling or directing it. Avoid interrupting students' thinking by giving immediate feedback. Later, you can give feedback privately or to the group as a whole. To time your feedback for greatest effect:

→ **Wait for a natural pause or stopping point.** For instance, if a few students have made insightful comments or followed the guidelines for using appropriate words and tone, you might say:

> "During those last few comments, I noticed that each of you used a friendly tone and one of the sentence starters we've been practicing. That made a meaningful contribution to our conversation."

→ **Take notes and give feedback later.** As you observe, note specific comments students make so that you can let them know later how and why their comments met the criteria you've set. Avoid publicly singling out one student for her contributions. Such public recognition can create a competitive environment, which may lead to students resenting each other or seeking your approval rather than advancing their conversations and learning.

Addressing Common Mistakes

As students learn these more advanced conversational skills, they'll inevitably make mistakes. Your skillful response can help them progress. Presume positive intentions, quickly get students back on track, and keep the conversations—and learning—going.

DISRESPECTFUL TONE

At times, a student may become so passionate about a topic that she asserts her opinions too harshly. Because students will often match your tone, try to keep your own tone calm as you respond.

→ **Let the student have a do-over.** Quickly help the student understand what she needs to fix and then give her a chance to do it.

> "Tia, try that again. Use a respectful tone and start with, 'I disagree because _____.'"

→ **Use a nonverbal or brief verbal reminder.** If you notice several students struggling with maintaining a respectful tone, set up a reminder system with them.

> "We've been so excited about our discussions lately that we've forgotten to always be polite even if we disagree. Who has a word or signal we can use to remind each other?"

Tips for Addressing Mistakes

✔ **Show empathy.** Use a neutral tone so students feel empowered to try again.

✔ **Give students a chance** to fix mistakes. Provide a new sentence starter or say what they need to do.

✔ **Use as few words as possible** and "quiet" body language, so everyone else stays focused on the topic, not the mistake.

Then, if needed, use the pre-established signal or word:

> "Scott, tone."

→ **Watch for changing social dynamics.** Be on the lookout for whether students are using agreement or disagreement to try to gain more social power. For instance, if you notice that one student is always disagreeing with only one other student, you may want to observe their social interactions throughout the day and then, if needed, privately revisit the purposes of disagreeing in academic conversations.

OVERLY SENSITIVE OR DEFENSIVE

Often students bristle when others challenge them. They may shut down, become upset, or talk back disrespectfully. Remember this is a very human response—we all want to feel accepted. To help students learn to keep these natural responses in check and stay focused on the conversation:

→ **Set students up for success.** Before a conversation that may be challenging, remind students of the importance of staying respectful and open-minded.

→ **Help students calm down.** Sometimes students may be too upset in the moment to process redirections rationally. In these moments, you might say:

> "Natalie, you seem upset. Take a minute to calm down. We'll talk later."

→ **Provide a replacement behavior.** If you think the student is calm enough to try again, coach him on how to do so.

> "Jermaine, let's try that again. Do you want to provide more evidence for your original statement? You might start with 'I still think _____ because _____ .'"

NOT GIVING REASONS OR EVIDENCE

Students may react too quickly to a statement—immediately agreeing, disagreeing, or challenging it without thinking. But, the rational reasons for their position may take much longer for them to express. To help these students:

→ **Validate their reaction.**

> "Desmond, you sound as if you feel strongly about that. Are you ready to provide your reasons, or do you need a few more minutes?"

→ **Give them time to think.**

> "Marco's statement seems to have inspired strong reactions in a few people. Turn and chat with your partner for a minute. See if you agree or disagree, and why."

→ **Guide them in clarifying their thoughts.** Sometimes students need help realizing exactly why they're agreeing or disagreeing. Be ready to give them specific guidance.

> "Do you disagree because of something we read in this chapter? Take a look again at page 42. I think it may have the evidence you're looking for."

SPEAKING TOO SOFTLY

Some students, either because they're shy or afraid of hurting a classmate's feelings, may hesitate to express disagreement or do so inaudibly. Try to steer clear of repeating their words, because that teaches students to depend on you. Our goal here is to help students speak effectively for themselves.

Instead, invite these students to repeat what they said. Of course, allow for exceptions to this general rule. Students learning to speak English, for instance, may want your help fully expressing their ideas.

Similarly, some students may be so shy that saying a word or two may be a struggle. Don't put these students on the spot by making them repeat themselves. Continue to provide individual practice and coaching for them.

Essential Skills at a Glance

AGREEING AND DISAGREEING	

Agreeing
(pages 141–148)
	→ Provide reasons and evidence that explain why you agree.
	
	→ Add on to someone else's statement:
	  • to give new reasons or new evidence
	  • to flesh out incomplete information

Disagreeing (pages 148–155)	→ Pause and evaluate the speaker's ideas first. → Challenge someone's ideas if you have valid doubts about the speaker's reasons or evidence. → Provide reasons and evidence for why you disagree. → Use an assertive but respectful tone and body language.
Partially Agreeing (pages 155–157)	→ Pause and evaluate the speaker's ideas first. → In your mind, sort out what you agree with and what you disagree with (or have questions about). → Be as clear and specific as possible.

Responding to Disagreements
(pages 157–161)
	→ Think about what the speaker said and decide how best to respond:
	  • Acknowledge the speaker and just keep listening.
	  • Stick with your position, and give additional reasons and evidence.
	  • Admit when you might be mistaken.
	  • Change your position and explain why.
	
	→ Use a respectful, nondefensive tone in responding.

Sample Letter to Parents

Dear Parents,

This week, we started working on some advanced conversational skills—how to respectfully agree and disagree. I know that even as an adult, I sometimes struggle with these skills, so I hope that by learning them at a much earlier age, your children will be more comfortable and confident exchanging ideas in school and beyond.

I'd like to share a few ideas for helping your child practice these skills at home if you'd like to do so:

- Have playful agree-disagree discussions. It's hard to practice these skills when emotions are heated, so look for fun ways to practice them. For instance say, "_____ is the best movie of all time." Challenge everyone present to come up with as many reasons as they can to support the statement. Then do the same for reasons to disagree with it.

- Offer encouragement when you notice your child trying to put these skills to use. For instance, if you see your child respectfully disagree with a sibling or friend, point out what he or she did well with that skill.

- Be a model. Children learn by example, so if they see us respectfully agreeing and disagreeing during our conversations they'll be more likely to use these skills themselves.

As always, please let me know if you have any questions or thoughts. Thank you for supporting your child's learning!

Letting Students Shine

Your role in students' conversations is critical—you can keep the learning on track, help students get unstuck, and make sure all voices are heard. As you become more adept in teaching academic conversation skills, you'll grow more comfortable in making moment-to-moment decisions about how you can best support students' learning. You'll know when students need your help to move the conversation forward, when to wait and see how things go, or when students need you to pause the conversation and help them reflect.

But, as you facilitate, be careful not to overdo it. The ultimate goal is for students to learn to talk with one another, not through you as the mediator, so as much as possible give students the spotlight and let their voices dominate. After all, they're the ones who are learning to think, speak, and listen. Plus, the more they know that their ideas and opinions are valued, the more invested they'll be in their learning and in the life of the classroom community.

Facilitating productive conversations also means you'll need to decide when to end them. We've all been in conversations that lasted just a few comments too long. Try to end before students tire of a topic, get frustrated with each other, begin repeating themselves, or otherwise disengage. By leaving on a high note, children will feel positive both about their skills and about the topic being discussed.

You also have a crucial role in giving students feedback as they progress. As you do, remember that listening closely and speaking effectively are challenging for all of us. Students' progress often occurs in fits and starts on their journey to achieving mastery. If you keep an eye out for the little successes students have,

you'll see signs of progress. And when you do, be sure to comment positively on all that they're doing well.

For those times when students misstep—because they will make mistakes, as we all do—use a light touch. Respectfully pause or stop the conversation, reflect on what happened, and keep moving forward. Sometimes a quick reminder of a sentence starter is all students need to get on track: "Feliz, try, 'The strategy I used for solving the problem was. . . .'" Or provide short prompting questions if a student remains stuck: "What happened first? Then what happened?"

Remember to provide support for yourself, too, especially if teaching academic conversation skills is new to you. Set realistic goals and try to team up with a colleague. Planning lessons together often makes tasks feel less daunting, and by working together you'll find more opportunities within the curriculum where you can fit in this teaching.

Finally, celebrate your own growth and successes. It's easy to focus on what didn't go well, but it's also vital to give yourself credit for lessons that seemed particularly strong and those moments when students put the conversational skills you taught to productive use.

Know that by taking the time to teach the language of learning, you're doing students a great service—guiding them to success in school and in their lives beyond school.

Quick Guide to the Teaching Techniques Used in This Book

This guide gives you a brief overview of some key techniques for teaching and having children practice the essential speaking and listening skills they need for academic success. Use it as a handy reference to support students' development of these skills.

TECHNIQUES FOR INTRODUCING A SKILL

Students are more likely to master speaking and listening skills when they can actively engage in learning them. The four techniques in this section are especially effective in fostering students' engagement.

Interactive Modeling

Unlike conventional modeling, Interactive Modeling gives students a clear mental picture of the skill being demonstrated, fully engages them in noticing details about that skill, and gives them immediate opportunities to practice and receive feedback. Interactive Modeling is also helpful for reteaching skills that students are struggling with or forgetting to use.

STEPS IN INTERACTIVE MODELING

1. **Say what you will model and why.** When teaching listening skills, you might say: "Careful listeners show with their faces and bodies that they're interested in what the speaker is saying. I'm going to show you how to do that. Watch and see what you notice."

2. **Model the behavior.** Have a volunteer summarize what she read during readers' workshop. Show interest by keeping eyes on the speaker, leaning forward, and perhaps nodding or smiling.

3. **Ask students what they noticed.** "What did you notice about how I showed I was listening with interest?"

4. **Invite one or more students to model.** "Who can show listening with interest like I just showed you?" Emphasize modeling the key skills students are expected to learn (in this lesson, eyes on speaker and leaning forward).

5. **Again, ask students what they noticed.** "What did you notice about how Sayani showed she was listening to me and interested in what I was saying?"

6. **Have all students practice.** "Turn and talk with your partner. Take turns describing what you read during readers' workshop. Show listening with interest the same ways that Sayani and I did." Again, emphasize practicing the skills that were modeled.

7. **Provide feedback.**

   → **Name the specific, positive actions you notice students doing.** For example: "Lots of you are looking at the speaker and nodding."

   → **Redirect if necessary.** For example: "Nickiya, turn your body toward Ari to show you're interested in what he's saying."

Fishbowl

In a Fishbowl, a small group of students (who have prepared in advance) hold a mock discussion to demonstrate the skills the class is learning. The rest of the class gathers around these demonstrators and observes them. Then the class names the key actions they noticed. Fishbowl is especially effective for showing more complex speaking and listening skills, how multiple skills look when used in combination, and how skills students have learned in one context (such as literature circles) look and sound in a new context (such as math).

Keys to success:

→ **Choose a familiar discussion topic that students will find engaging.** They'll have an easier time following the flow of the conversation and tuning in to the speaking and listening skills being shown.

→ **Keep the Fishbowl discussion focused and brief** (no more than five minutes).

→ **Choose students carefully but inclusively.** You'll need students who will be able to competently and publicly demonstrate the skills with a little pre-coaching from you, but refrain from having the same students demonstrate again and again. You want observers to recognize that everyone can be successful with the skills. Over the course of the year, try to give all students chances to participate as Fishbowl demonstrators.

→ **Prepare the students who will be in the Fishbowl ahead of time.** Your class's learning will be only as strong as the demonstration itself, so be sure those in the Fishbowl can demonstrate the skills as you want students to use them. From time to time, you may want to include yourself in the Fishbowl to demonstrate a certain skill or to ensure that the conversation keeps flowing.

→ **Tell the class what to watch for in the Fishbowl demonstration.** Prompt them to notice what specific, positive actions those in the Fishbowl show. For example: "Your classmates will be demonstrating asking relevant and respectful questions. Watch and see exactly how they do that."

→ **Set up guidelines for the class to follow as they describe their observations** once the Fishbowl demonstration has ended, such as speaking with respect and pointing out the positives. Then, before beginning this debriefing, remind students of the guidelines. For example: "How are we going to show respect to each other as we talk about our observations of the Fishbowl?"

Expert Demonstration

Watching adults or older students competently use a set of skills gives students a clear vision of where they're headed—and the hope and confidence that they, too, can reach such a high level. You can invite colleagues, guests, or older students to present a live demonstration of the conversational skills you're teaching or use a video recording of people demonstrating the skills.

Use the Expert Demonstration strategy to teach more complex skills, such as paraphrasing, or to show how multiple skills work in combination, such as asking and answering questions and agreeing with what others said. Like the Fishbowl, this technique is also helpful for showing how skills learned in one area (reading) can apply in another (science).

Keys to success:

→ **Keep the demonstration or clip brief.** The shorter it is, the more likely students will notice the key skills.

→ **Choose a familiar topic or text.** If students have to work hard to understand the content of the demonstration, they won't be able to focus on the skills. You can also find captivating examples of speaking skills in action in literature, history, or the news. For example:

- *Present brief clips* of political talk shows or famous speeches to older students so they can see how speakers use their tone of voice and body language.

- *Use children's books* such as the Mo Willems's Pigeon series to teach the same skills to younger students.

→ **Connect with former students.** If you can, enlist some of your former students as live "experts" for the demonstration. Check with their current teachers to make sure the scheduling will work. Or ask colleagues who teach older grades about other students who could model and might benefit from the collaboration.

→ **Use open-ended questions** to help guide students in pointing out the key skills being shown. For example: "How did the demonstrators use the skills of adding on to what a previous speaker said?" Follow up as needed: "Why was that important? How did their voices sound? What made that respectful?"

→ **Avoid pointing out what the demonstrators did yourself.** Students' learning will be more powerful if they make these connections themselves.

→ **Repeat parts of the clip or demonstration** as needed to have students notice additional skills or details.

→ **Videotape students once they become proficient at using the skills demonstrated.** For example, videotape students paraphrasing what another student said about a read-aloud. Then use that same read-aloud and video clip with next year's class to show the skill in use.

Focused Brainstorm

In a Focused Brainstorm, you describe a situation ("Let's say we're discussing my solution to a problem in science") and ask students to brainstorm ways to use a certain skill in that situation ("How might you respectfully say that you disagree with my solution?"). Then let students come up with ideas of their own to use as they practice. A Focused Brainstorm is particularly useful in teaching students more complex skills such as using reasons and evidence, and works best when students have some experience with a skill but need a little extra guidance to deepen their understanding.

Steps:

→ **Briefly introduce the situation and skill.** For instance, to help students brainstorm possible questions to ask a classmate, you might begin by saying, "Suppose I just shared about a science experiment I had conducted and described my results. What are some questions you could ask me that would be thoughtful and help everyone learn more about what I did?"

→ **Record students' ideas in chart form.** This chart will give students ideas of sentence starters, questions, or topics to use in future conversations. You can also use the chart for further teaching. For instance, you might want students to classify the types of questions, such as those seeking clarification and those seeking more information.

→ **Remind children of the expectations, such as being respectful *and* staying on topic.** For instance, if a student says, "I got different results. Are you sure you did it the right way?" you might respond, "Delaney, try to reframe that question in a respectful way that's focused on my experiment. I'm going to give you a starting phrase, 'Can you tell us more about how you . . . ?'"

→ **Reflect, summarize, and clarify.** Once students have brainstormed a sufficient number of ideas, guide them to reflect on what their ideas have in common and how they can help them in future conversations.

→ **Provide guided practice.** Give students an immediate chance to practice the skills with a partner or small group in the context of a specific academic lesson. For instance, you might send students off to take turns briefly describing science experiments and asking focused, respectful questions. Circulate during this practice so you can provide coaching and positive feedback. Remind students to continue practicing the skills in future conversations.

TECHNIQUES FOR PRACTICING A SKILL

To become fluent with speaking skills, students need a great deal of practice. Although that practice can be as simple as turning and talking with a partner, you can mix and match the fourteen different ideas that follow to target specific speaking and listening skills or to make practice more engaging.

Circle Map

Use this structure, which can also be a helpful graphic organizer, for practice with more complex speaking and listening skills, such as being precise in word choice and distinguishing fact from opinion.

→ **Place students in groups.** Give each group a chart-sized piece of paper and markers.

- **One student in each group draws a large circle around a small inner circle.** Another student lists the group's assigned topic or big idea in the inner circle. For instance, if students are working on using evidence to support main ideas for a social studies unit on immigration, the big idea might be "People move to new places for many different reasons."

- **Students brainstorm text-based evidence statements that support the big idea** and list them in the outer circle. For example: "In the 1800s, people emigrated for better economic opportunities" and "For centuries, people have moved in search of greater religious freedom."

- **After a few minutes, tell students to stop brainstorming.** Have groups switch charts and then discuss each other's work.

Four Corners ··························

Four Corners is a powerful strategy for quickly grouping students according to their preferences or opinions. You can use it to spark discussions about a variety of topics and to give students a chance to discuss topics either with partners or in a small group.

- **Pose a question to the whole group and provide four possible responses.** Designate one corner of the room for each response. For older children, each corner could represent one of four opinions on a current event ("Which of the following do you think our city should make a priority—build a new stadium so we can have a professional sports team, give tax breaks to a private business to build a new stadium, put money into developing our libraries instead of a new stadium, or build a new stadium and raise taxes to support libraries?"). For younger children, each corner could represent one of four aspects of studying a topic, such as animal habitats ("Which habitat did you read about that most interested you—desert, ocean, savannah, or plains?").

- **Students go to the corner of their choice** (or, if needed, assign students to a corner).

- **Once in the corner, students discuss the response their corner represents.** Students can do this in pairs or as a small group in each corner.

→ **Specify which speaking skills you want students to focus on.** For instance, "As you talk with one another, remember to use complete sentences the way we've been practicing."

→ **After a few minutes, invite students to share examples** of how they used the speaking skills in their discussions. To extend this activity, have students go to different corners and repeat the process.

Info Exchange ⋯⋯⋯⋯⋯⋯

This structure is well suited for practicing how to talk about the evidence that supports an opinion or idea. Students receive only small bits of information at a time and start to build an understanding of the opinion or idea on the basis of this evidence.

→ **Before the lesson, prepare strips of paper,** each with one fact or one statement from a text. For instance, each slip might contain a quotation from a particular text, or each might be a fact about an animal the class has been studying. Animal slips might say, "This animal lives in the ocean," "This animal is a mammal," and "This animal travels in pods."

→ **Distribute the slips so that each student has one.** It's OK if some of the slips are the same. Direct students to find a partner (or assign partners).

→ **Partners read their statements to each other.** Then they switch statements and find new partners.

→ **Direct students to continue the process,** finding new partners and swapping statements each time.

→ **After a few minutes, signal for students' attention.**

→ **Invite students to state conclusions based just on the evidence that they read and heard.** You could do this in pairs, small groups, or the whole group. For example, if students were exchanging facts about an animal, they might talk with a partner about which animal they believe it is and explain how the evidence supports their view.

Inside-Outside Circles ....

This simple conversation structure gives students a chance to talk with several different partners and move around as well.

- → **Have students count off by twos.** The ones stand and form an inner circle, facing outward. Each two stands and faces a one, creating the outer circle.

- → **Give students an engaging topic to discuss.** Remind them of the speaking or listening skills to practice. For example: "With your partner, try to summarize the key events that happened in chapter four of our read-aloud book."

- → **After two or three minutes, signal for quiet attention.** Have a few students share what they and their partner discussed.

- → **To change partners, have students in each circle take one step to their right.** Give them a new topic to discuss: "With your new partner, discuss how chapter four builds on the earlier chapters we've read. Use evidence from each chapter to explain your ideas. Remember to agree and disagree respectfully." Change partners one or two more times, using a new question or topic each time.

Maître d'··

Maître d' gives students a chance to move around and practice with a variety of partners in a fast-paced way.

- → **Tell students that you are the maître d'** at a pretend restaurant and will call out tables for a certain number of customers, such as "Table for three." Students will then form groups of that number.

- → **Once groups are formed,** give them an engaging topic to discuss that's connected to the content they're learning. For example, students at each "table" can discuss how many shapes can be formed by combining three different types of triangles, or whether a particular object might float or sink. Prompt them to use whatever speaking or listening skill you want them to practice. For instance, "Remember to back up what you are predicting with sound reasons and evidence."

→ **Give students a few minutes to talk** and then call out "Table for" a different number. Students quickly reform into groups of that number, finding new people to talk with.

→ **Remind students that one goal of this practice is inclusion,** so if the table numbers do not work out evenly, it's OK for one or two groups to have different numbers of participants. Before giving students topics to discuss, you may want to give them practice in forming groups quickly so that they get a feel for how this structure works.

Numbered Heads Together

This structure can provide students with a strong motivation for practicing listening skills because anyone in the group may be called on to report what the group discussed.

→ **Assign students to small groups of four or five,** and have students count off within each group.

→ **Give the groups an intriguing topic to discuss** and remind them of the listening skills to practice. For example, you might have students work together to solve a math problem and remind them to look at the speaker and show interested listening. Each member of the group has to be ready to present the steps his or her group came up with for solving the problem.

→ **Allow several minutes for students to "put their heads together"** for an in-depth discussion of the topic.

→ **Signal for quiet attention,** and then call out a number (for example, two).

→ **The person from each group with that number** (that is, each two) reports out by summarizing what his or her group discussed.

→ **Repeat,** calling out different numbers each round.

Paired Verbal Fluency ....

This structure is especially effective for practicing the skills of backing up what one has to say with evidence and agreeing and disagreeing respectfully.

⟶ **Place students in pairs.** Partners decide who is A and who is B (or you decide for them).

⟶ **Give the topic for discussion** and tell students what speaking skills you want them to practice. For example, you might have students respond to a passage they just read in science or social studies: "Each of you will talk to your partner for one minute about what you just read—things you found interesting, surprising, or questionable, and why. Then you'll each have thirty seconds to respond to what your partner said. When you respond, be sure to use our sentence frames to express agreement, partial agreement, or disagreement."

⟶ **First A speaks for one minute.** Then B speaks for one minute.

⟶ **Each student has thirty seconds to respond** to what the other said.

⟶ **To conclude,** A and B each get twenty seconds to summarize what their partner said or express their last thoughts.

Popcorn ....

This structure enables students to practice speaking to a whole group and natural turn-taking (that is, waiting for a natural pause in the conversation to speak instead of raising hands and being called on). Popcorn can be especially helpful for practicing speaking with confidence and using complete sentences. Tell students what they'll be sharing about and choose a topic they've been reading, studying, or discussing.

⟶ **Students sit in a circle.** When they're ready to share, they "pop up" (stand) and state their idea. They don't raise hands and you don't call on people to speak. After the student who popped up speaks, she remains standing. For instance, you might have students share one word, phrase, or sentence from the Declaration of Independence that they think is particularly effective. One student might pop up and say, "Life, liberty, and the pursuit of happiness." Another might stand up and recite, "Our repeated Petitions have been answered only by repeated injury."

→ **If two people pop up at the same time,** they sit back down and try again for a single pop.

→ **If one student shares an idea that another student (who's still sitting) also has in mind,** that student pops up in silent agreement with the speaker.

Pros and Cons ······················

This structure is specifically designed so that students can practice making and responding to arguments with logical reasons and supporting evidence. Students are assigned a position to argue, rather than choosing their own, so they can stay focused on reasons and evidence rather than their personal feelings or opinions.

→ **Place students in pairs.** Have them decide who is A and who is B (or you decide for them). Designate A as "pro" and B as "con."

→ **Read aloud a challenging opinion** based on something your class has been reading or studying. For instance: "It was OK for the wolf to blow down the first two little pigs' houses" or "Students should not be able to use calculators to solve math problems at school."

→ **Give everyone one minute to think.** Then, each pair debates as follows:

- The "pro" person has one minute to list all the reasons for her side.

- The "con" person then has one minute to do the same.

- Both students then have thirty seconds to respond to the other person's statement, supporting their ideas with evidence.

→ **Debrief with the whole class,** focusing on which reasons and evidence were most compelling for each side.

Say Something

This structure gives students practice in essential speaking skills such as how to stay on topic and speak concisely. It can also help students develop a deeper understanding of a topic and reinforce listening and attention skills.

- **Place students in pairs.** Have them read a small portion of a text or watch or listen to a short video or audio clip.

- **At a natural break in the text or clip,** each student in the pair says one thing (a question or comment) about what they read, heard, or saw. What they say does not have to relate to what their partner said, nor should they respond to each other's question or comment.

- **Students repeat this process** until the text or clip is completed. Students may then have an open conversation about the entire text or clip and respond to any of their partner's earlier questions or comments.

Swap Meet

This structure allows students to practice with a variety of partners in quick succession. It's especially helpful for sharing answers to open-ended questions and for practicing essential speaking skills, such as staying on topic.

- **Pose a question** to the class. For instance: "What evidence can you find in this chapter to support the author's conclusion that insects can be helpful to humans? Review the chapter and list your ideas."

- **Students find a partner** (or assign partners) and swap one idea. You may also want to have students add any new ideas they hear to their list.

- **Students find another partner and repeat the process.** Continue for a few more rounds.

- **Optional:** Gather all students back together and let them share what they learned from others.

This, That, Neither, Both

This structure is especially helpful when students are working on advanced conversation skills such as expressing agreement, partial agreement, or disagreement.

- ↪ **Have students form a circle.** Use a string or long strip of tape to divide the circle into halves.

- ↪ **Read two opinion statements about a topic** your class has been studying. Designate each half of the circle to represent one of the statements. For instance, if a class has been studying food and nutrition, the statements might be "Junk food should be banned from schools" and "Restaurants should have to list the ingredients and calories in their foods."

- ↪ **On your signal,** students move to a certain area of the circle as follows:
  - If they agree with both statements, they stand in the middle of the circle.
  - If they agree with only one statement, they move to the appropriate half of the circle.
  - If they disagree with both statements, they stand outside the circle.

- ↪ **Have students find a partner.** You might tell them to find someone who made the same choice that they did, or someone who made a different choice. Instruct them to brainstorm as many reasons and facts as they can to support their opinions.

- ↪ **Call on a few students to share** the reasons and facts for their opinions. Let students change positions in the circle if they're persuaded to change their opinions. Repeat as time allows.

20 Questions

This take on the classic guessing game gives students practice asking and answering questions in a fun way. It's also effective for reviewing content students have been studying.

- ↪ **Pair students up** or place them in small groups if you want them to come up with the questions to ask cooperatively.

→ **Designate yourself or a student to lead the game.** That person then thinks of a specific person, place, event, or topic that students have been studying. For instance, the leader might say, "I'm thinking of a three-digit number" or "I'm thinking of a character from a book we have read this year."

→ **The class can ask up to 20 questions** to try to figure out what the person, place, event, or thing is. Place parameters on the types of questions that can be asked, such as:

- only "yes-no" questions, or no "yes-no" questions
- questions that start with a specific question word (*what, where, when, who, why, how*)
- questions that can be answered in just one sentence

→ **Students may guess at any time.** However, after two incorrect guesses, the leader reveals the answer.

→ **Name another student to lead** and repeat as time permits.

Venn Diagram

This structure is helpful in practicing respectful agreement and disagreement, backing up main ideas with reasons and evidence, and choosing precise words.

→ **Pair students up and give each pair a blank circle Venn diagram.** One partner's name goes at the top of one circle, the other's at the top of the other circle.

→ **Give students a series of opinion statements based on their classwork.** Statements could be about their views of this work: "I think writers' workshop is more fun than math" or "I think nonfiction is more interesting than fiction." Statements could also be about the content of the work, such as "We should spend more money to study space" or "We should rid the world of invasive weeds." If both students agree, they write that statement in the middle of the diagram. If only one does, he writes the statement in the appropriate circle. If neither does, they write the statement on the outside of the diagram.

→ **For each statement,** students briefly discuss their reasons and evidence.

→ **Each pair then joins with another pair** to compare notes and continue the conversation.

TECHNIQUES FOR PROVIDING ONGOING SUPPORT

Even with the best initial teaching and practice, students will likely need concrete and ongoing support in building their academic conversation skills. Below are some simple but powerful supports. Don't be afraid to use them frequently and for as long as students show they still need them.

Just as importantly, be sure to remove the supports as soon as students no longer need them. For instance, once students are proficient with showing the physical signs of listening, take down anchor charts showing how listening looks. Similarly, remove sentence starters for agreeing and disagreeing once students no longer need them.

Anchor Charts

These charts are especially helpful when students are first learning a new skill or are struggling in an area you previously thought they had mastered. Once you've taught a set of skills, post a chart summarizing the key points. Refer to these charts before students begin a discussion and when you notice students needing support during a discussion.

> **Question Words**
> * Who * When
> * What * Where
> * Why * How

Tips:

→ **List what to do** rather than what not to do.

→ **Use as few words as possible.** Highlight only the most important aspects of the skills.

→ **Consider using photographs** of your students demonstrating the skills.

Notes

Notes on owl pellets:
—furry
—round
—dark brown to black
—firm but soft enough to rip
—smell like soil

Often students forget a great idea when they start to speak. They may especially struggle when they're first learning more complex speaking skills, such as how to add details, cite concrete evidence, or build on to conversations. In these situations, being able to bring notes of key ideas to the conversation can help. For example, during science you might have students make notes of their observations to share as part of a whole-class reflection.

Tips:

→ **Teach what the notes should look like.**

→ **Use index cards,** small pieces of paper, or sticky notes so that students have room to write only key ideas.

→ **Direct students to place the cards behind them** until it's their turn to speak so they can focus on listening.

If students need extra support, add a practice component: Have them make notes with you or a family member on a topic, practice speaking with their notes at hand, and then use the notes during the actual classroom conversation.

Sentence or Question Starters

Getting started is often the hardest part of speaking. To help with this task, provide students with sentence or question starters (or stems). This kind of support is especially helpful when children, particularly English language learners, are just beginning to learn these skills.

Tips:

→ **Begin with one sentence starter for everyone to use,** and then add more as time goes on, or provide a variety of sentence starters and let students choose one. For example:

- "I solved the problem by _____."

- "I observed _____, and so I concluded _____."

→ **Even when most of your students** no longer need sentence or question starters for a certain skill, keep them handy for students who still benefit from using them.

Shared Responsibility With a Partner ·······················

Practicing listening and speaking skills with a partner help students reach mastery. For instance, when practicing remembering what a speaker said, students can turn to a partner, combine their memories, and double-check their thinking before they share with the larger group.

Tips:

→ **Teach students how to work with partners.** (Interactive Modeling, page 172, is effective for this teaching.)

→ **Assign and vary partners frequently.** From time to time, pair struggling students with more skilled students, who can serve as models and provide positive support as well. However, be sure these skilled partners also have plenty of chances to work with those who will challenge them and help them further develop their own skills.

Teacher Prompts and Facilitation ·······················

You may want to more directly guide conversations in ways that prompt students to use certain skills, especially when they're first learning them. For example, if students are working on the skills of agreeing, adding on, and disagreeing, you might use prompts such as:

"Does anyone want to add on to what _____ said?"

"Does anyone want to agree with _____ and provide further evidence, or disagree and give reasons why?"

Tips:

→ Think carefully about when and how to give prompts. Provide support as needed, but also strive to make conversations flow as naturally as possible.

→ Give individual or small-group coaching to students who need extra practice in the same area. You may want to revisit why the skill matters, be more explicit about how it looks and sounds in action, and provide some more closely guided practice.

→ Be a whisper coach. If a student is struggling with a skill in a whole-group setting, sit by her during the next whole-group discussion. Lean over and quietly give her some sentence starters, connections to make, or other ideas for how she can take part in the conversation.

Suggested Timeline

When to Teach Speaking and Listening Skills

Here's a sample timeline you can use as a starting point for planning when to introduce various speaking and listening skills over the course of the year.

	Weeks 1–4	Early to Middle of Year	Middle to End of Year
Kindergarten	→ Focusing attention → Showing interest → Taking turns	→ Sustaining attention → Developing listening comprehension skills → Speaking confidently → Core question skills	→ Staying on topic → Speaking with clarity → Asking purposeful questions → Answering questions
Grades 1–2	→ Focusing attention → Showing interest → Taking turns → Speaking confidently	→ Sustaining attention → Developing listening comprehension skills → Staying on topic → Speaking with clarity → Core question skills → Answering questions	→ Asking purposeful questions → Organizing thoughts → Distinguishing facts from opinions → Presenting evidence → Agreeing → Disagreeing
Grades 3–4	→ Focusing attention → Showing interest → Sustaining attention → Taking turns → Speaking confidently → Core question skills	→ Developing listening comprehension skills → Staying on topic → Speaking with clarity → Asking purposeful questions → Answering questions → Organizing thoughts → Distinguishing facts from opinions	→ Presenting evidence → Persuading others → Agreeing → Disagreeing → Partially agreeing → Responding to disagreements

CONTINUED ▶

	Weeks 1–4	Early to Middle of Year	Middle to End of Year
Grades 5–6	→ Focusing attention → Showing interest → Sustaining attention → Taking turns → Speaking confidently → Core question skills → Organizing thoughts	→ Developing listening comprehension skills → Staying on topic → Speaking with clarity → Asking purposeful questions → Answering questions → Distinguishing facts from opinions → Presenting evidence → Agreeing → Disagreeing	→ Persuading others → Partially agreeing → Responding to disagreements

Tips:

→ **During the first few weeks of school,** teach foundational skills, such as how to listen when someone else is speaking and how to take turns, as part of establishing basic classroom routines and expectations. Once students master these beginning skills, introduce new skills in the following weeks as stand-alone lessons or as part of academic lessons.

→ **As you set up academic lessons,** think about how to integrate the teaching of speaking and listening skills into them. For instance, you could teach the skills of asking questions during a science lesson about observing an object from nature.

→ **If you begin your school day with a morning meeting,** use part of that time to help students learn and practice specific speaking and listening skills. Then, during a closing circle or other end-of-the-day routine, have students practice those skills again as they reflect on their learning for the day.

About the *Responsive Classroom*® Approach

All of the recommended practices in this book come from or are consistent with the *Responsive Classroom* approach to teaching—a research-based approach to elementary education that leads to greater teacher effectiveness, higher student achievement, and improved school climate. *Responsive Classroom* practices help educators develop competencies in three interrelated domains: engaging academics, positive community, and effective management.

To learn more about the *Responsive Classroom* approach, see the following resources published by Northeast Foundation for Children and available from www.responsiveclassroom.org ▪ 800-360-6332.

Classroom Management: Set up and run a classroom in ways that enable the best possible teaching and learning.

> *Interactive Modeling: A Powerful Technique for Teaching Children* by Margaret Berry Wilson. 2012.

> *What Every Teacher Needs to Know*, K–5 series, by Margaret Berry Wilson and Mike Anderson. 2010–2011. (Includes one book at each grade level.)

> *Teaching Children to Care: Classroom Management for Ethical and Academic Growth K–8*, revised ed., by Ruth Sidney Charney. 2002.

Morning Meeting: Gather as a whole class each morning to greet one another, share news, and warm up for the day ahead.

> *The Morning Meeting Book*, 3rd ed., by Roxann Kriete and Carol Davis. 2014.

> *80 Morning Meeting Ideas for Grades K–2* by Susan Lattanzi Roser. 2012.

> *80 Morning Meeting Ideas for Grades 3–6* by Carol Davis. 2012.

Doing Math in Morning Meeting: 150 Quick Activities That Connect to Your Curriculum by Andy Dousis and Margaret Berry Wilson. 2010. (Includes a Common Core State Standards correlation guide.)

Doing Science in Morning Meeting: 150 Quick Activities That Connect to Your Curriculum by Lara Webb and Margaret Berry Wilson. 2013. (Includes correlation guides to the Next Generation Science Standards and *A Framework for K–12 Science Education*, the basis for the Standards.)

Morning Meeting Messages K–6: 180 Sample Charts from Three Classrooms by Rosalea S. Fisher, Eric Henry, and Deborah Porter. 2006.

99 Activities and Greetings: Great for Morning Meeting . . . and other meetings, too! by Melissa Correa-Connolly. 2004.

Morning Meeting Professional Development Kit. 2008.

Doing Morning Meeting: The Essential Components DVD and viewing guide. 2004.

Sample Morning Meetings in a Responsive Classroom DVD and viewing guide. 2009.

Positive Teacher Language: Use words and tone as a tool to promote children's active learning, sense of community, and self-discipline.

The Power of Our Words: Teacher Language That Helps Children Learn, 2nd ed., by Paula Denton, EdD. 2014.

Teacher Language for Engaged Learning: 4 Video Study Sessions. 2013.

Teacher Language Professional Development Kit. 2010.

Teacher Language in a Responsive Classroom DVD. 2009.

Teaching Discipline: Use practical strategies, such as rule creation and positive responses to misbehavior, to promote self-discipline in students and build a safe, calm, and respectful school climate.

Teasing, Tattling, Defiance and More: Positive Approaches to 10 Common Classroom Behaviors by Margaret Berry Wilson. 2013.

Rules in School: Teaching Discipline in the Responsive Classroom, 2nd ed., by Kathryn Brady, Mary Beth Forton, and Deborah Porter. 2011.

Responsive School Discipline: Essentials for Elementary School Leaders by Chip Wood and Babs Freeman-Loftis. 2011.

Teaching Discipline in the Classroom Professional Development Kit. 2011.

Creating Rules with Students in a Responsive Classroom DVD. 2007.

Foundation-Setting During the First Weeks of School: Take time in the critical first weeks of school to establish expectations, routines, a sense of community, and a positive classroom tone.

The First Six Weeks of School by Paula Denton and Roxann Kriete. 2000.

The First Day of School DVD. 2007.

Learning Through Academic Choice by Paula Denton, EdD. 2005.

Guided Discovery in a Responsive Classroom DVD. 2010.

Classroom Organization: Set up the physical room in ways that encourage students' independence, cooperation, and productivity.

Classroom Spaces That Work by Marlynn K. Clayton with Mary Beth Forton. 2001.

Movement, Games, Songs, and Chants: Sprinkle quick, lively activities throughout the school day to keep students energized, engaged, and alert.

Closing Circles: 50 Activities for Ending the Day in a Positive Way by Dana Januszka and Kristen Vincent. 2012.

Doing Math in Morning Meeting: 150 Quick Activities That Connect to Your Curriculum by Andy Dousis and Margaret Berry Wilson. 2010. (Includes a Common Core State Standards correlation guide.)

Doing Science in Morning Meeting: 150 Quick Activities That Connect to Your Curriculum by Lara Webb and Margaret Berry Wilson. 2013. (Includes correlation guides to the Next Generation Science Standards and *A Framework for K–12 Science Education*, the basis for the Standards.)

Energizers! 88 Quick Movement Activities That Refresh and Refocus, K–6, by Susan Lattanzi Roser. 2009.

99 Activities and Greetings: Great for Morning Meeting . . . and other meetings, too! by Melissa Correa-Connolly. 2004.

Morning Meeting Activities in a Responsive Classroom DVD. 2008.

16 Songs Kids Love to Sing (songbook and CD) performed by Pat and Tex LaMountain. 1998.

Preventing Bullying at School: Use practical strategies throughout the day to create a safe, kind environment in which bullying is far less likely to take root.

How to Bullyproof Your Classroom by Caltha Crowe. 2012. Includes bullying prevention lessons.

Solving Behavior Problems With Children: Engage children in solving their behavior problems so they feel safe, challenged, and invested in changing.

Sammy and His Behavior Problems: Stories and Strategies from a Teacher's Year by Caltha Crowe. 2010. (Also available as an audiobook.)

Solving Thorny Behavior Problems: How Teachers and Students Can Work Together by Caltha Crowe. 2009.

Teasing, Tattling, Defiance and More: Positive Approaches to 10 Common Classroom Behaviors by Margaret Berry Wilson. 2013.

Working With Families: Hear parents' insights, help them understand the school's teaching approaches, and engage them as partners in their children's education.

Parents & Teachers Working Together by Carol Davis and Alice Yang. 2005.

Child Development: Understand children's common physical, social-emotional, cognitive, and language characteristics at each age, and adapt teaching to respond to children's developmental needs.

Yardsticks: Children in the Classroom Ages 4–14, 3rd ed., by Chip Wood. 2007.

Child Development Pamphlet Series (based on *Yardsticks* by Chip Wood; in English and Spanish). 2005 and 2006.

To Learn More:

Visit **www.responsiveclassroom.org** for additional information about the *Responsive Classroom* approach to teaching elementary students, including the strategies discussed in this book, free articles, blog posts, and video clips from real classrooms.

Resources From Other Publishers

Accountable Talk® Sourcebook: For Classroom Conversation That Works by Sarah Michaels, Mary Catherine O'Connor, Megan Williams Hall, and Lauren B. Resnick. University of Pittsburgh. 2010.

Academic Conversations: Classroom Talk That Fosters Critical Thinking and Content Understandings by Jeff Zwiers and Marie Crawford. Stenhouse. 2011.

Classroom Discourse: The Language of Teaching and Learning by Courtney B. Cazden. Heinemann. 2001.

Opening Minds: Using Language to Change Lives by Peter H. Johnston. Stenhouse. 2012.

Talking About Text: Guiding Students to Increase Comprehension Through Purposeful Talk by Maria Nichols. Heinemann. 2008.

Talking Classrooms: Shaping Children's Learning Through Oral Language Instruction, edited by Patricia G. Smith. International Reading Association. 2000.

ACKNOWLEDGMENTS

While I was working on this book, I had the joy of hearing Chip Wood speak. In several presentations, he talked about how important it is for teachers to create space for students to talk to each other and find their voices. Chip has always been an inspiration, but the passion, insights, and knowledge he offered in these talks came at just the right time for this book. Thanks also to Ruth Charney, Marlynn Clayton, and Paula Denton, whose writing and work on behalf of children have had such a profound influence on me as a teacher and on my conversations with students. They are never too far from me when I write.

I also want to thank the readers who gave input along the way. Reader feedback is important for every book project, but that was especially true for this book, as we were trying out new formats and ideas. Kerry O'Grady was refreshingly honest and helpful before I even started to write. Her observations about what readers might need stayed with me and guided me throughout the writing process. Thanks also to my colleague Babs Freeman-Loftis and the other readers, Lynn McKay, David Murray, and Kate Umstatter, for all their insights, ideas, and suggestions. The book is so much richer, more useful, and more accessible as a result of their feedback.

As always, thanks to Jim Brissette and Alice Yang, whose vision and insights into the topic of student conversations and what will help teachers teach them kept me focused and grounded as I wrote. Their revisions, additions, comments, and questions always make me a better writer. Thanks also to Elizabeth Nash and Cathy Hess for their meticulous copyediting and proofreading work. And I'm running out of words to thank Helen Merena for the artistry she brings to our books. She makes them both beautiful and so much easier to read, and I always enjoy my writing more once it's passed through her capable hands.

I also want to express my appreciation to Mary Beth Forton, for her frequent encouragement of my writing and feedback on this and all my writing projects, and Lora Hodges, our executive director, for her enthusiasm and interest in this book, as well as for her inspiring words in the foreword.

As ever, thanks to Kathy Woods, Babs Freeman-Loftis, and Lara Webb for their cheerleading, kindness, and support. I also want to acknowledge the powerful influence of my family. Among other things, my parents and six siblings first introduced me to the necessity of being able to make and defend a strong argument. And thanks to Andy and Matthew whose conversations make every day richer and happier.

Finally, thanks to each and every student I taught. You were always my best teachers and are now my writing inspiration.

ABOUT THE AUTHOR

 **Margaret Berry Wilson** has been using the *Responsive Classroom* approach to teaching since 1998. She worked for fifteen years as a classroom teacher in Nashville, Tennessee, and San Bernardino, California. In 2004, Margaret became a *Responsive Classroom* consultant with Northeast Foundation for Children, presenting *Responsive Classroom* workshops and coaching educators throughout the country. She currently serves as an assistant head of school in Riverside, California, where she resides with her husband, Andy, and their son, Matthew.

Margaret is the author of a number of books published by Northeast Foundation for Children, among them *Teasing, Tattling, Defiance and More: Positive Approaches to 10 Common Classroom Behaviors* (2013); *Interactive Modeling: A Powerful Technique for Teaching Children* (2012); *Doing Math in Morning Meeting: 150 Quick Activities That Connect to Your Curriculum* (with co-author Andy Dousis; 2010); and *Doing Science in Morning Meeting: 150 Quick Activities That Connect to Your Curriculum* (with co-author Lara Webb; 2013).

INDEX

agreeing and disagreeing, skills of
    common mistakes when learning, 165
    and connections to Common Core,
        137
    essential components of
        agreeing thoughtfully, 141
        disagreeing respectfully, 148
        expressing partial agreement, 155
        responding to disagreements, 157
    Essential Skills at a Glance (table), 168
    Expert Demonstration, as technique
        for introducing, 145
    Fishbowl, as technique for
        introducing, 142, 145, 159
    importance to student learning, 136
    Interactive Modeling, as technique for
        introducing, 141, 149, 153, 155, 157
    parent letter about (sample), 169
    tips for effective teaching of, 140
arguments, skills in crafting
    common mistakes when learning, 128
    and connections to Common Core,
        103
    essential components of
        distinguishing facts from opinion,
            113
        persuading others, 122
        presenting evidence, 119
        speaking in an organized way, 107
    Essential Skills at a Glance (table), 132
    Expert Demonstration, as technique
        for introducing, 122
    Fishbowl, as technique for
        introducing, 116, 122
    importance to student learning, 102
    Interactive Modeling, as technique for
        introducing, 107, 111, 114
    parent letter about (sample), 133
    tips for effective teaching of, 106

checking in, as listening comprehension
    skill, 27
Circle Map, 117
    description of, 177
Common Core Connections, 7, 41, 71, 103,
    137

disagreeing. See Agreeing and
    disagreeing

evidence
    criteria for convincing presentation
        of, 119
Expert Demonstration
    description of, 175
    See also entries for specific skills

feedback, tips on providing
    for agreeing and disagreeing, 162
    for asking and answering questions,
        92
    for crafting arguments, 125
    for listening, 30
    for speaking, 61
Fishbowl
    description of, 174
    See also entries for specific skills
Focused Brainstorm
    description of, 176
    See also entries for specific skills
Four Corners, 15, 144
    description of, 178

Info Exchange, 48
    description of, 179
Inside-Outside Circles, 15, 19, 48, 58, 76,
    90, 120, 144, 156
    description of, 180

Interactive Modeling
  description of, 172
  steps of, 173
  See also entries for specific skills

listening skills
  common mistakes when learning, 33
  and connections to Common Core, 7
  essential components of
    developing comprehension, 25
    focusing attention, 12
    showing interest, 17
    sustaining attention, 20
  Essential Skills at a Glance (table), 36
  Expert Demonstration, as technique
    for introducing, 18, 23, 27
  Fishbowl, as technique for
    introducing, 23, 27
  importance to student learning, 6
  Interactive Modeling, as technique for
    introducing, 12, 14, 16, 20, 22, 25
  parent letter about (sample), 37
  tips for effective teaching of, 10

Maître d', 15, 59, 78, 124, 144
  description of, 180

Numbered Heads Together, 29, 83, 124
  description of, 181

Paired Verbal Fluency, 23, 159
  description of, 182
paraphrasing, 27
  use of sentence starters with, 28
parent letters, samples of, 37, 67, 98, 133,
  169
Popcorn, 49
  description of, 182
Pros and Cons, 26, 123, 160
  description of, 183

question words, 79
questions, skills in asking and answering
  common mistakes when learning, 95
  and connections to Common Core, 71
  essential components of
    asking purposeful questions, 79
    asking questions respectfully, 77
    differentiating questions from
      statements, 75
    giving high-quality answers, 85
  Essential Skills at a Glance (table), 97
  Expert Demonstration, as technique
    for introducing, 77, 89
  Fishbowl, as technique for
    introducing, 77, 79, 89
  Focused Brainstorm, as technique
    for introducing, 82
  importance to student learning, 70
  Interactive Modeling, as technique
    for introducing, 75, 85, 87
  parent letter about (sample), 98
  tips for effective teaching of, 74

reinforcing language, 62. *See also*
  Feedback, tips on providing

Say Something, 52, 55
  description of, 184
sentence starters
  for adding on, 147
  when agreeing, 145
  when disagreeing, 152
  for paraphrasing, 28
  when partially agreeing, 156
  for presenting facts and opinions,
    114–115
  for putting events in order, 113
  when responding to disagreement,
    161
  and using complete sentences, 59

speaking skills
    common mistakes when learning, 63
    and connections to Common Core, 41
    essential components of
        speaking confidently, 50
        speaking with clarity, 56
        staying on topic, 53
        taking turns, 45
    Essential Skills at a Glance (table), 66
    Expert Demonstration, as technique
        for introducing, 54, 60, 64
    Fishbowl, as technique for introducing,
        48, 52, 60, 64
    Focused Brainstorm, as technique
        for introducing, 53, 57, 58, 59
    importance to student learning, 40
    Interactive Modeling, as technique for
        introducing, 45, 47, 50, 55, 56, 58, 64
    parent letter about (sample), 67
    tips for effective teaching of, 44
summarizing, 27
Swap Meet, 17, 55, 58, 88, 154
    description of, 184

This, That, Neither, Both, 151
    description of, 185

20 Questions, 49, 81
    description of, 185

Venn Diagram, 150
    description of, 186

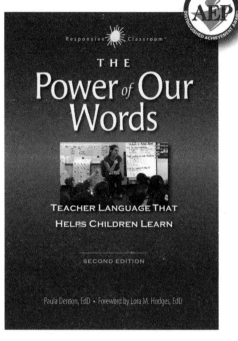

ABOUT THE PUBLISHER

Northeast Foundation for Children, Inc., a not-for-profit educational organization, is the developer of *Responsive Classroom*®, a research-based approach to elementary education that leads to greater teacher effectiveness, higher student achievement, and improved school climate. *Responsive Classroom* practices help educators develop competencies in three interrelated domains: engaging academics, positive community, and effective management. We offer the following resources for elementary school educators:

Professional Development Services

→ Workshops for teachers and administrators (locations around the country and on-site)

→ On-site consulting services to support implementation

→ Resources for site-based study

→ National conference for school and district leaders

Publications and Resources

→ Books and videos for teachers and school leaders

→ Professional development kits for school-based study

→ Website with extensive library of free articles: www.responsiveclassroom.org

→ Free newsletter for elementary educators

→ The *Responsive*® blog, with news, ideas, and advice from and for elementary educators

For details, contact:

Responsive Classroom®

Northeast Foundation for Children, Inc.
85 Avenue A, P.O. Box 718
Turners Falls, Massachusetts 01376-0718

800-360-6332   www.responsiveclassroom.org
info@responsiveclassroom.org